**NEVI**

## THE OWLS

C000098751

Trev,

Happy Birthday!.

All the best,

Dom.

# NEVER MIND THE OWLS

## The Ultimate SHEFFIELD WEDNESDAY

## QUIZ BOOK

## ANDREW CLARK

FOREWORD BY JOHN PEARSON

The History Press

First published 2013

The History Press
The Mill, Brimscombe Port
Stroud, Gloucestershire, GL5 2QG
www.thehistorypress.co.uk

British Library Cataloguing in Publication Data.
A catalogue record for this book is available from the British Library.

ISBN 978 0 7524 9781 5

Typesetting and origination by The History Press
Printed in Great Britain

# Contents

# Acknowledgements

**F**irstly, I'd like to say a huge thank you to Michael Bullivant for his invaluable support and advice throughout the production of this book (and also congratulate him on being the first person to complete the quiz!).

I'd also like to thank John Pearson for being kind enough to provide the foreword and Sheffield Wednesday Football Club for all of their help and support.

Finally, a big thank you to Anita, Elinor and Daniel for all of their help with the book and also for putting up with me in general.

All images have been reproduced with the kind permission of Sheffield Wednesday FC, Bradford City FC, Blackburn Rovers FC, Nottingham Forest FC, Oldham Athletic FC, Wigan Athletic FC, the FA and the Football League.

# Foreword

## by John Pearson
(Sheffield Wednesday 1980–85)

I t was a great pleasure to be asked to write the foreword for this book, as Sheffield Wednesday Football Club has always been such a big part of my life. I was born into a family of Wednesdayites and have been firmly immersed in the club pretty much from the moment I was born.

As a youngster I lived just a stone's throw from Hillsborough and one of our neighbours was Owls midfielder Tommy Craig, who lodged just a few doors down from our house. From my school playground we could actually see the Wednesday players during their training sessions and, like most boys in our school, I dreamed that one day it would be me donning one of the famous blue and white striped shirts.

I was a season ticket holder at Hillsborough from an early age. As I was born at the start of September the perfect birthday present for me each year was always a Wednesday season ticket and my dad used to take me to all of the home games, as well as some of the away fixtures. I have some fantastic memories of me and my dad watching Wednesday throughout the 1970s.

Ironically, though, my dad did not get to see my Wednesday first team debut. I was thrown into the fray unexpectedly at the tender age of just 17 years and 12 days, to replace Terry Curran who had been suspended following his dismissal at Oldham Athletic in September 1980. However, while I was making my bow against Bristol City at Hillsborough, my dad was holidaying in Majorca and only found out that I'd played and scored when the British Sunday newspapers finally made it out to the Balearic Islands a couple of days later!

I played all four games while Terry was suspended and managed to score in each of them, which not only included my home League debut against Bristol City, but also my away League debut at Swansea City, and my League Cup debut against Watford. To complete the set, I then scored on my FA Cup debut later that season at Newcastle United.

My five seasons with Wednesday were a fantastic time for me and I feel privileged to have played professional football for the team that I have supported since I was a kid. Indeed, I'm still lucky enough to be involved with the club today and have always been extremely proud to be associated so strongly with Sheffield Wednesday.

I'm sure, like me, all Owls supporters will very much enjoy testing their knowledge of our great club with this terrific little quiz book. It's fetched back some wonderful memories and I've even learnt a thing or two about the club as well. I hope you all enjoy grappling with the questions as much as I did and that the book brings back as many great memories for you as it did for me.

All the very best to all Owls fans.

# Introduction

**A**lthough I suppose the book's title might have attracted the odd confused ornithologist, I'm pretty much assuming that the vast majority of people who read this book are fellow Sheffield Wednesday supporters. So, a warm welcome to this light-hearted quiz book to one and all of you (and, if you are a confused ornithologist, then good luck answering the questions).

Sheffield Wednesday fans obviously come in many different shapes and sizes, and it's exactly the same with the questions in this book. There are long ones, short ones, the odd really hard one, and even a few frivolous ones, particularly towards the end of the book.

The book has been split into 30 rounds and most of them have 11 questions, which obviously cleverly mirrors the number of players in a football team! In addition, there is one extra question in each round – a kind of 'super-sub' if you like – designed to provide that extra slice of excitement.

There are no fixed rules on how you should complete the questions. You can do them on your own, in competition with your mates or as a team; you can write the answers down or shout them out – it's entirely up to you!

Each of the questions, along with the answers, has been constructed solely by me using information that is believed to be correct up to September 2013. All of the information included in the questions has been meticulously researched using a wide variety of sources, including old programmes, a number of books, the internet and the staggering knowledge of one of my mates.

However, I'm sure that there will be some debate over the authenticity of some of the facts and figures that have been included. In fact, whilst writing the book, I did find that some statistics that ought to be indisputable, for instance the age of a player when he made his debut, can actually vary from one source to another.

This is not an excuse for laziness. Every fact contained in the book has been checked, double-checked and then triple-checked. If any errors, however minor, have crept in, then I do apologise profusely – but please don't let that spoil your enjoyment of the book.

I've thoroughly enjoyed both researching and writing this book, and reminiscing about Wednesday games and players from a bygone era. And I hope that you get as much pleasure from reading the book as I did from writing it. Enjoy!

**Andrew Clark**

# Round

# 1

# 'Hark Now Hear, the Wednesday Sing...'

Let's kick off with a round that's guaranteed to stir the passions of every Wednesdayite – 11 questions that focus on encounters with our oldest and bitterest of foes, Sheffield United. The Sheffield derby is one of English football's longest-running rivalries, with the first competitive fixture between Wednesday and United dating back to 1893, and it remains one of the country's most fiercely contested clashes. So I know this round will provoke strong feelings but try to rein in those emotions and keep your cool as we go head-to-head with the Blades…

1   Which Wednesday player scored at both Hillsborough and Bramall Lane in the 2011/12 season Steel City derbies?

2   In the 2008/09 season, the Owls famously completed the double over United for the first time in 95 years. Whose 25-yard thunderbolt proved to be the decisive goal in the return game at Bramall Lane?

3   Over the last decade, the Sheffield derby has been a
    regular fixture on the footballing calendar, but how many
    times did Wednesday and United contest League matches
    during the 1980s?

4   The Owls' leading post-war goal scorer in Sheffield
    derbies bagged five goals in just four appearances against
    the old foe during the early 1960s. Can you name him?

5 Only four competitive fixtures between Wednesday and United have finished goalless, and two of those were in the same League campaign. Do you know in which season both Steel City derbies ended in scoreless draws?

6 The 'Boxing Day Massacre' in 1979 saw us record our biggest ever victory over the Blades. What other record was set that day?

7 And which four players scored for the Owls in that glorious Boxing Day triumph?

8 Another one to savour: which two players scored our goals in the 2–1 FA Cup semi-final victory over the Blades in 1993?

9 By all accounts, the 1900 FA Cup second round replay between Wednesday and United was a brutal affair. How many players were still on the pitch at the end of 90 minutes?

10 Lloyd Owusu's place in Sheffield derby folklore was secured during our home clash with the Blades in September 2002. Why?

11 And finally, Alan Quinn holds a unique distinction in terms of Steel City derbies. What is it?

## FACT OR FICTION?

*Wednesday have never been beaten by the Blades in a Premier League fixture.*

# Round 2

# Hello, Goodbye...

Although as fans we stick with our club through thick and thin, the group of players who wear the blue and white stripes is inevitably in a fairly constant state of flux. That's obviously the way it has always been – as fresh faces join the club, familiar ones move on to pastures new. Indeed, while the introduction of the transfer window may have limited the number of months when players are free to move, the transfer merry-go-round remains very much in full swing. This round looks at those comings and goings, testing your knowledge of the Hillsborough arrivals and departures lounge over the past four decades…

1   Let's kick off with a relatively easy one: which legendary Wednesday defender was signed by Ron Atkinson in December 1989 from IFK Gothenburg for a bargain fee of just £375,000?

2   Which misfiring forward did 'Big Ron' offload to West Bromwich Albion as part of the deal that saw Carlton Palmer arrive at S6?

3   And which player left Wednesday to join Celtic as part-funding for Paolo Di Canio's grand arrival in 1997?

4 Last transfer makeweight: which Owls striker headed to Crystal Palace as part of the deal that brought Mark Bright to the club in September 1992?

5 Wednesday legend Lee Bullen arrived at Hillsborough on a free transfer in the summer of 2004, but from which Scottish club did he join us?

6 And from which West Yorkshire club did we sign Jermaine Johnson during the final days of the January 2007 transfer window?

7 During Jack Charlton's reign, two influential players arrived at S6 from Everton; a midfielder in 1981 and a central defender in 1982. Can you name either player?

8 Viv Anderson and Danny Wilson both left Hillsborough in the summer of 1993 to form a new management team at which club?

9 During the 2011/12 season, both Ryan Lowe and Mike Jones joined Wednesday from which League One team?

10 And from which Yugoslavian outfit did David Pleat sign both Darko Kovacevic and Dejan Stefanovic in 1995?

11 Finally, two defenders left Hillsborough to join Chelsea during the second half of the 1990s. Name either of them.

## OWL-A-GRAM

*Unscramble the letters to find the name of a Trevor Francis big-money signing who didn't quite live up to his billing:*

### DON'T SAY INN

# Cosmopolitan Owls

Football has changed a lot from when I first started going to Hillsborough, with one of the most obvious changes being the influx of foreign players. Over the past couple of decades, the English game has taken on an increasingly cosmopolitan look, and Wednesday have embraced this trend with a whole host of foreign nationals strutting their stuff on the Hillsborough turf; some more successfully than others. Anyway, see how you get on with this set of questions which all relate to Owls who were born beyond the UK's shores…

1   The first player to win a full international cap for a country outside of the British Isles and Ireland while playing for Wednesday was a silky midfielder who spent five seasons at Hillsborough in the second half of the 1980s. Can you name him?

2   Which Algerian central defender enjoyed a short but successful stint at S6 during the first half of the 2006/07 season before instigating a big-money move to Premier League Charlton in the January transfer window?

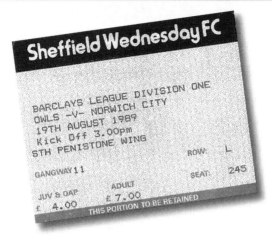

3   Reda Johnson has played international football for which
    country?

4   And for which country did former Owls midfielder Petter
    Rudi play international football?

5   Which Czech Republic international goalkeeper
    competed with Kevin Pressman for the Wednesday
    keeper's jersey during our final two seasons in the
    Premier League?

6   Only one Swede has ever won the Owls 'Player of the
    Year' award. Can you name him?

7   Not one to dwell on for too long, but which hapless
    Swede made 16 appearances in the Wednesday goal after
    arriving at Hillsborough from Stockport County in the
    summer of 2003?

8   Which Congolese forward scooped the Owls 'Player of
    the Year' award after topping the club's scoring charts
    with ten goals during the 2003/04 campaign?

9   And which Dutch striker was our leading goal scorer
    in each of the first three seasons of the twenty-first
    century?

10  'I thought I knew everything about English football, but I
    had never heard of a team called Wednesday or a place
    called Sheffield'. Which import from the US came out
    with this less than flattering comment following his S6
    arrival in 1990?

11  Finally, which Spanish starlet scored on his Owls debut
    against Birmingham City in August 2012, before leaving
    the club after only six months of his season-long loan?

## FACT OR FICTION?

> *Pelé twice played against Sheffield Wednesday at
> Hillsborough but did not score on either occasion.*

# Round

# 4

# The Last is the First

It's time for a novelty 'pub-quiz' round now, just to keep you all on your toes. But don't worry, the title actually sounds far more complicated than it really is. Quite simply, the last letter of each answer is the first letter of the next answer, and so on. Get the first question right and there'll be no stopping you! To make life slightly easier, all of the answers are the surname of a former or current Wednesday player. So get your glasses filled and enjoy this traditional pub-quiz favourite.

1   Goalkeeper who made over 200 appearances after arriving at S6 in 1967, following a unique exchange deal that saw his brother move in the opposite direction.

2   Dutch midfielder signed by David Pleat in August 1996. Managed three goals in 19 appearances in his only season with the Owls before returning to Holland.

3   Towering centre half who wears a black headguard and scores from 30 yards.

4   Striker who spent six weeks on loan at Hillsborough in autumn 2005. No goals in eight appearances hardly

suggested we had a future England international in our midst, but apparently we did.

5   Became Wednesday's record signing when he moved from Stoke for £70,000 in 1966. Scored 45 goals in three seasons before moving back to the Potters in a cut-price deal.

6   Elegant midfielder who graced Hillsborough during two spells in the 1960s and '70s; probably best to gloss over his 'useless' managerial stint though.

7  Dutch winger who spent three seasons with us after moving from Vitesse in 2007. Scored five goals, including a memorable 25-yard free kick at Bramall Lane in September 2009.

8  First choice right-back throughout the '80s; Brazilian nickname and 49 goals made him an all-time Hillsborough legend.

9  Belgium international striker who joined the Owls in a big-money move from PSV in 1999. His initial promise soon faded as we slid out of the Premier League and he eventually left on a free transfer after two frustrating seasons.

10  Attacking midfielder who made a positive impact during his half-season loan stint in 2005/06. Subsequently enjoyed success at both Burnley and Bolton.

11  American defender who spent five seasons at Hillsborough after joining on a free transfer in 2005. His commitment to the cause and assured defensive displays made him a firm fans' favourite.

## OWL-A-GRAM

*Unscramble the letters to find the name of a dependable Wednesday defender:*

### FIRST FIT HELPER

# In the Beginning

Let's get it out of the way, the round you've all been dreading, the one about the history of the club. I can feel the beads of perspiration starting to build on your forehead but don't panic, it's not going to be like resitting your History GCSE. In fact, don't even see it as an exam, more of a gentle meander through the fascinating early years of our great club. You never know you might actually know some of the answers and, even if that's not the case, don't worry you won't be made to re-sit the 'test' later in the book!

1   Right, let's kick off with the obvious question: in which year was the club formed?

2   And in which year were Wednesday elected to the Football League?

3   What was the name of our first permanent home ground?

4   We took up residence at Hillsborough in 1899; but what was the ground originally called?

5   What was the name of the first trophy that Wednesday ever won?

6   We've reached the FA Cup final six times in total, but on how many of those occasions did we actually win the trophy?

7 And how many times have we been crowned Football League Champions?

8 A tough one now: what was unusual about our 4–1 victory over Aston Villa during the 1898/99 campaign?

9 Which Wednesday player is widely acknowledged to have been the first professional footballer in England?

10 The club's all-time leading goal scorer is a Scot who racked up 216 League and Cup goals during his illustrious 20 years with Wednesday in the early twentieth century. What's his name?

11 Finally, in which year was the club's name officially changed from 'The Wednesday' to 'Sheffield Wednesday'?

## FACT OR FICTION?

*Sheffield Wednesday FC is the oldest football club in Sheffield.*

# 6

# I'll Name that Owl in One!

When I was asked to write this book, my first thought was I'll have to include a fitting tribute to the genius quiz-show host Tom O'Connor. So here it is! You'll be given five clues to the identity of a Wednesday player, either past or present, and you simply have to say who it is in as few clues as possible. So go on, name that Owl in one!

## Player A

1   Came through the club's youth ranks and was named Academy 'Player of the Year' in the 2004/05 season.

2   Made his Wednesday first-team debut in a 1–1 draw with Reading at Hillsborough in April 2006.

3   His goal against Plymouth in April 2008 was voted Sky Sports' Championship Goal of the Season.

4   Scored after just 45 seconds in our famous Steel City derby victory at Bramall Lane in February 2009.

5   Left-back who made more than 200 Owls appearances before moving to Doncaster Rovers in 2011.

### Player B

1  Scored on his Owls debut at Newcastle United in April 1969 when aged just 18.

2  Fearless centre forward whose ten seasons at Hillsborough were beset by injury problems.

3  Named Wednesday's 'Player of the Year' in 1974, despite ending the season with a broken leg.

4  Scored our first goal in third-tier football, and topped our scoring charts in both 1970/71 and 1975/76.

5  Nicknamed 'Prendo', he made over 200 appearances and netted 59 times during his Owls career.

### Player C

1  Bought himself out of the army in order to pursue a career as a professional footballer.

2  Signed by Trevor Francis from Aston Villa in 1994.

3  Netted twice on his first two Owls outings: at Everton on Boxing Day and against Coventry two days later.

4  Featured regularly for Wednesday, either in midfield or attack, between 1995 and 1998.

5  Made his name at Fratton Park and still holds Portsmouth's record for most goals in a season.

### Player D

1  Born in Jarrow in 1936; made his Owls debut as a striker at Blackpool in March 1957.

2  Scored Wednesday's first ever goal in European football during the 1961 Inter-Cities Fairs Cup tie in Lyon.

3  Won one England cap in 1964 following his positional switch from striker to defensive duties.

4    Spent his whole career with the Owls, making almost 350 appearances over 15 seasons.

5    Sadly, best remembered for a costly error that led to Everton's winning goal in the 1966 FA Cup final.

## Player E

1    Born in Newport on the Isle of Wight in December 1983.

2    Began his career with Portsmouth making his Pompey first-team debut in August 2001.

3    Arrived at S6 on loan from Stoke City in October 2008 making the move permanent in January 2009.

4    A versatile defender who has made over 150 League appearances for the Owls.

5    Voted Wednesday's 'Player of the Year' in 2012/13.

## Player F

1    England international signed by Howard Wilkinson in September 1985.

2    Scored his first Owls goal after coming off the bench against Nottingham Forest in December 1985.

3    Perennial substitute during his three seasons at S6, with over half of his appearances coming from the bench.

4    Was described during his early Stoke City days as the most exciting prospect since Stanley Matthews.

5    His son is following in his footsteps, playing professional football in the top-flight (with Arsenal) and for England.

## OWL-PHABET

*The surnames of three Owls 'Player of the Year' recipients in the 1980s begin with an 'S'. Name them.*

# Round 7

# Wednesday Till We Die!

As dour, down-to-earth Yorkshire folk, the Wednesdayite psyche has always been strong on doom and gloom – if you assume the worst then at least you won't be too disappointed, or so the theory goes. So when I asked a fellow Wednesdayite what topics to cover in this book, I shouldn't have been too surprised with his first suggestion: 'You'll have to include a round on relegation seasons; us Wednesday fans like nothing better than torturing ourselves with that sort of thing,' he said, before eulogising about last day defeats that sent us down. So, by popular demand, here it is – a round of questions covering our relegation skirmishes, although, be warned, not all of them do end up in abject misery!

1   Let's kick off with our most recent heartbreak: failure to beat which team condemned the Owls to relegation from the Championship on the final day of the 2009/10 season?

2   The 1989/90 campaign also ultimately ended in despair as Ron Atkinson's side disproved the old adage that some teams are too good to go down. Which side defeated us at Hillsborough on the last day of that season and who won their final game to save their skins at our expense?

3 Another Hillsborough final day of despair now: defeat to which team on a wet Wednesday evening in April 1970 condemned the Owls to relegation from the top tier of English football?

4 Relegation battles have not always ended in final-day despondency though: in the 1975/76 season, we needed to win our last game to avoid sliding into the old Fourth Division. Which team did we defeat in that vital game to preserve our third-tier status?

5 We also managed to beat the drop on the last day of the 1973/74 season. Who did we beat on the final day of that campaign to secure our safety, and who scored the only goal of the game?

6 Of all our relegation escapes, the 1927/28 campaign was the most spectacular, with the Owls avoiding the drop despite being seven points adrift at the foot of the table with ten games to go. Which legendary skipper deservedly received much of the credit for spearheading that 'Great Escape'?

7   Much more recent one now: who scored our first goal against Middlesbrough on the final day of 2012/13 that set us on the way to victory and banished any relegation fears?

8   Which Wednesday manager holds the unfortunate record of suffering the most relegations during his time at the Hillsborough helm?

9   In the 1999/00 season, a dismal start ensured that we were languishing in the Premier League relegation zone for the whole campaign. How many matches was it before our first League victory that season?

10   Danny Wilson was dismissed before the end of the ill-fated 1999/00 campaign. Who was in temporary charge of team affairs when we officially lost our Premier League status following a 3–3 draw at Arsenal in May 2000?

11   And finally, let's go out on this fiasco: the 1974/75 season saw us record our lowest ever League points tally as we slipped into the third tier of English football for the first time. How many goals did we muster in total during the final 17 games of that dismal campaign?

## OWL-A-GRAM

*Unscramble the letters to find the name of a Wednesday striker whose ten League goals were not enough to prevent relegation in 1989/90:*

### ASK A LION AND NIT

# Bouncing Owls

Although it does go against the grain, even I feel that we need an antidote after the despair and anguish of the previous round. So, it's time for a more uplifting round, quite literally, as this set of questions focuses solely on our promotion-winning campaigns. And we certainly have had our fair share of promotion glory down the years. Sit back and enjoy revelling in all of those successes as you tackle this set of illustrious questions.

1    Latest promotion campaign first: who did Wednesday beat on the final day of the 2011/12 season to secure a return to Championship football?

2   In the 1990/91 season, our return to the top flight
    was clinched with a 3–1 Hillsborough victory in the
    penultimate game of the season. Can you remember the
    opponents and which star striker bagged two of the goals
    that day?

3   Promotion to the old First Division in 1983/84 was sealed
    with four games to spare. Who scored from the penalty
    spot in the 1–0 home victory over Crystal Palace that
    secured our top-flight return?

4   In 1949/50, the Owls were promoted back to the top tier
    after clinching second place on goal average. Who was
    the unfortunate team that finished third with the same
    number of points as us but missed out on promotion
    glory by 0.008 of a goal?

5   Two Wednesday managers have guided the club to
    top-flight promotion during their first seasons in the
    Hillsborough hot-seat. Can you name either of them?

6   And which manager has led the Owls to promotion on
    the most occasions?

7   Which father and son combination have both captained
    Wednesday to promotion glory during Second Division
    Championship-winning seasons?

8   And which central defensive colossus skippered us to
    promotion success in the 1983/84 season?

9   Only one player has ever finished two successful
    promotion campaigns as Wednesday's leading goal scorer.
    Can you name the prolific striker who achieved this feat
    during the 1950s?

10  A Welsh midfielder won the Owls 'Player of the Year' award for his performances during the 1979/80 promotion-winning season. Can you name him?

11  And which striker was voted 'Player of the Year' after topping our scoring charts during the 2004/05 promotion-winning campaign?

## OWL-PHABET

*The surnames of four players who appeared for Wednesday in a Premier League fixture begin with the letter 'N'. Can you name them?*

# Connect Four

Right, time for another more traditional type of quiz round. Don't worry, it's not too complicated. All you have to do is find the answers to the first four questions and then work out the connection between each of your answers. I've spent hours checking that there is only one genuine connection but, if you do come up with a better connection, give yourself a point – for instance, if you know for a fact that each player's mother-in-law has the middle name 'Dave', you've got the point! Actually, you wouldn't because the connections do all have to be Owls-related. Anyway, good luck!

## Connect 1

1   Arrived at S6 in 1990 after a fractious 11 months in the Loftus Road hot-seat. Perhaps most famous for being the country's first £1 million footballer.

2   Northern Irish midfielder who won the League Cup with Luton Town and then with us. More recently turned to the dark side, although perhaps undercover!

3   A self-imposed Hillsborough exile and change of allegiance didn't diminish the love and affection Wednesday fans hold for this truly legendary man.

**Sheffield Wednesday FC**

```
*********************************
*RUMBELOWS LEAGUE CUP SEMI FINAL*
*********************************

        OWLS - V - CHELSEA

   WEDNESDAY  27th FEBRUARY  1991
         KICK - OFF  7.45pm

             SOUTH  STAND
BLOCK   GANGWAY  ROW   SEAT        PRICE

  J        8      N    208    9.00/6.0
         THIS PORTION TO BE RETAINED
```

4    Popular Hillsborough goalkeeper who was too short for Big Jack's liking. Also enjoyed success with both Sunderland and Manchester United in the 1980s.

*So, what's the connection between this gang of four?*

## Connect 2

1    Club record transfer fee was paid to secure the services of this lanky midfielder in 1989. More recently featured in a Paddy Power advert emerging from a bath in his Wednesday kit.

2    One of the club's greatest ever full-backs who graced the Hillsborough turf throughout the 1960s; his son proved to be a chip off the old block.

3    Moved to Hillsborough on a free transfer from Manchester United in 1991. First black footballer to be capped by England at full international level.

4 Wednesday legend from the 1930s nicknamed 'The Man with the Fluttering Feet'. His surname is the name of a common British bird (feathered variety!).

*And what connects these four players?*

## Connect 3

1 Popular Geordie forward from the first half of the 1970s; memorably scored a hat-trick against Crystal Palace in an FA Cup fourth round replay at Villa Park in 1973.

2 Diminutive striker who topped the club's scoring charts during all three of the seasons he spent in S6 during the early 1980s.

3 Blond-haired central defender from the mid-1990s; achieved cult status after scoring against the Blades in a memorable 3–1 Hillsborough victory in 1994.

4    Distinguished Northern Ireland international who played left-back for a couple of seasons in the early 1970s; a robust style of play earned him the nickname 'Tank'.

*And what has this group of four got in common?*

## Connect 4

1    Aptly described as a nomadic journeyman forward, but his Owls 'Player of the Year' award in 1985 clearly shows he was so much more than that to Wednesday fans.

2    Red-haired defensive Owls midfielder who Brian Clough once suggested 'Couldn't trap a bag of cement' shortly after the Forest boss had signed him in the summer of 1984!

3    Central defender who started out at Hillsborough and won a Championship winners' medal with Leeds in 1992; enjoyed the best spell of his career as Norwich captain, despite leading the Canaries to relegation.

4    Highly regarded centre-half from the early 1960s who many shrewd observers felt would have gained the ultimate honour with England in 1966 but for one naive misdemeanour.

*And finally, what's the connection between these four former Owls?*

## TAKE FIVE

*Only five men have played over 150 Premier League matches for the Owls. Can you name them?*

# Who Scored
# the Goal?

A more straightforward round now: all you have to do is name
the player who scored the goal – it's exactly what it says in the
title! Listed below are 11 Wednesday fixtures from the past four
decades, with details of our opponents, the ground the game
was played at, the date, the competition and the final score. The
answer to each question is quite simply the player who scored
our goal or, in two cases, goals, in that particular game. To give
you a clue to each scorer's identity, the number of letters in
his name along with a couple of those letters has also been
provided. So go on, who scored the goal?

| 1 | Fulham | Hillsborough | 28 August 2012 | League Cup | 1-0 |
|---|---|---|---|---|---|
| | | G_ _ _ | _A_ _ _ _ | | |
| 2 | Sheffield United | Hillsborough | 19 October 2008 | Championship | 1-0 |
| | | _ _ _ V_ | W_ _ _ _ _ | | |
| 3 | West Bromwich Albion | The Hawthorns | 13 April 2007 | Championship | 0-1 |
| | | _E_ _ | B_ _ _ _ _ | | |

| 4 | Newcastle United | St James' Park | 14 April 1984 | Second Division | 0-1 |
|---|---|---|---|---|---|
| | | _ A_ _ | S_ _ _ _ _ _ | | |
| 5 | Manchester United | Old Trafford | 1 January 1985 | First Division | 1-2 |
| | | I _ _ _ | _A_ _ _ _ | | |
| 6 | Manchester United | Hillsborough | 9 November 1985 | First Division | 1-0 |
| | | _ E _ | C_ _ _ _ _ _ | | |
| 7 | Manchester United | Hillsborough | 21 March 1987 | First Division | 1-0 |
| | | _A_ _ _ | _ _ _ _T | | |
| 8 | Aston Villa | Villa Park | 18 January 1992 | Premier League | 0-1 |
| | | _I_ _ _ | J_ _ _ _ _ | | |
| 9 | Leeds United | Elland Road | 4 March 1995 | Premier League | 0-1 |
| | | _H_ _ _ | _ _ _ _ _E | | |
| 10 | Arsenal | Hillsborough | 26 September 1998 | Premier League | 1-0 |
| | | _ _ E | _ _ _ _ _ _E | | |
| 11 | Sheffield United | Hillsborough | 1 November 2000 | League Cup | 2-1 |
| | | _F_ _ | E_ _ _ _ | | |

## OWL-A-GRAM

*Not a prolific scorer, but can you unscramble the letters to find the name of this Wednesday stalwart whose goal secured a 1–0 victory over Norwich City in January 1993:*

## NOT THIN GINGER OWL

# Round 11

# Just About Managing

It's time for a round on the gaffers now. These are the men who hold the destiny of our club in the palm of their hands even though, just like us, they can sometimes only look on with anguish at the hapless performances of their highly-paid charges. Like all clubs, we've had our fair share of managerial heroes along with a few pantomime villains thrown in for good measure, but how much can you remember about the men at the Hillsborough helm? Oh yes, and before I forget, the answers do not include caretaker-managers. Good luck!

1   Appointed in 1891 as secretary-manager, who was Wednesday's first and longest serving manager?

2   And which Owls boss holds the record for the shortest period in charge?

3   Which manager boasts the highest proportion of wins during his time at the Hillsborough helm?

4   We've had a lot of managers down the years, but only one of them has had two spells in permanent charge of our club. Can you name him?

5   Which manager did Wednesday infamously sack on Christmas Eve?

6   And who was sacked after securing a 1–0 victory over the Blades?

7   Which manager took charge of his first Wednesday game during the 1995 Intertoto Cup campaign?

8   The club has hired two Welsh-born managers. Can you name either of them?

9   Who was the club's manager when the Owls were relegated to the third tier of English football in 2003?

10  And who was in charge when we bounced back with promotion to the Championship two seasons later?

11  Finally, which Wednesday boss has led the club out at Wembley on the most occasions?

## OWL-PHABET

*The surname of four former Wednesday managers begins with a 'W'. Can you name them all?*

# Three Lions on a Shirt

Although it may be unimaginable to young Owls fans, there was a time when players from our club regularly represented the national side. Indeed, across the 1990s, six Wednesday players featured in the England team, while in the '60s three once appeared in the same line-up and back in the '30s we even had four players in a number of England starting XIs. Furthermore, an Owl played for England in the first ever international match. In fact, the more I think about it, it's probably fair to say we've virtually carried the national side for most of the last 140 years! Anyway, see how you get on with this lot.

1   Let's get the nineteenth-century question out of the way first: who was Wednesday's first ever international footballer?

2   And who was the last Wednesday player to win a full England cap during his time at Hillsborough when he played at left-back against Bulgaria in 1998?

3   The last Owl to score a goal for the full England team was a midfielder who bagged his only international goal against San Marino in 1993. Can you name him?

4    David Hirst scored one goal in three England outings.
     Against which country did he score?

5   Three Wednesday players featured in the England team against Luxembourg in September 1961. Can you name any two of them?

6   The club record for consecutive England appearances is 26, set between 1928 and 1933. Which legendary Owls full-back holds this record?

7   Two Wednesday players started all three of England's 1992 European Championship matches in Sweden. Who were they?

8   England's 1992 Euros squad also included two players who moved to Hillsborough the following summer. Name them.

9   Which Wednesday goalkeeper was put on stand-by for England's 1986 World Cup finals squad?

10  And which legendary Owls winger was included in England's 1954 World Cup finals squad, although he did not play in any of the games?

11  Three Wednesday players who featured during the 2012/13 campaign had all won full England caps prior to their S6 arrival. Can you name any two of them?

## OWL-A-GRAM

*Unscramble the letters to find a former England international and Owls favourite:*

### DREW AS CHILD

# It'll be 'Owl' Right on the Night

Like most Yorkshire men, I'm firmly entrenched in the 'glass half empty' camp, so writing this round on mishaps and misfortunes was not too distressing for me. However, if you are a bit squeamish or suffer from a nervous disposition, then it might be better to look away now. The rest of you enjoy this ghoulish collection of calamitous capers.

1   Who missed a penalty and was booked before half-time on his Owls debut at Oldham in August 2012?

2   What dubious footballing feat did Owls' midfielder Paul McLaren accomplish in the 1–1 draw at Leicester City in March 2003?

3   Which Wednesday player entered the record books in August 2000 for receiving the fastest red card in English football history?

4   The Owls were involved in a bizarre record set in a
    League game at Craven Cottage in January 1961. What
    was the record?

5   Jeremy Helan infamously received two bookings but
    was not sent off in a League game at Huddersfield in
    December 2012. Who was the referee and which player's
    shirt number did he mistakenly record for the first
    infringement?

6  A former Hillsborough star was sent off while making his Barnsley debut ironically against the Owls in December 2003. Name the player.

7  What unwanted club record did Norman Curtis, Vince Kenny and Eddie Gannon set during Wednesday's First Division clash with West Bromwich Albion in December 1952?

8  Referee Jack Taylor was at the centre of controversy during our Second Division game at Bolton Wanderers in September 1974. Why?

9  During the 1977/78 season, Wednesday set a new club record when ten different players did what?

10  Carlton Palmer holds a unique record relating to the five Premier League teams that he played for. What is it?

11  Not one to dwell on for too long but, after leading Wolves 3–0 in a fourth round FA Cup penalty shoot-out in 1995, we somehow managed to lose the tie. Who, almost inevitably, missed our final penalty?

## FACT OR FICTION?

*A Wednesday player scored the fastest ever own goal in English top-flight football history.*

# Wednesday Wonderland

Right then, time for me, and probably most of you, to indulge ourselves with a round on the highpoint of my time as a Wednesday fan – our last Cup success. It might be almost a quarter of a century ago, but I'm sure most of you will remember our triumphant cup run of 1991 as if it was yesterday. And it was the big one, the League Cup, or whatever it was called back then.

1    Let's kick off with a nice easy one: who scored the only goal in the 1991 League Cup final?

2    And what was the competition called in the 1990/91 season?

3    The trophy was not presented by a traditional 'dignitary'. Who did present it?

4    Three Wednesday players started all ten games during our victorious League Cup campaign. Can you name any two of them?

5 And which Owl suffered Wembley heartache, missing the final through suspension after playing in all of the other matches throughout the Cup campaign?

6 We all know that our League Cup run culminated in a 1–0 Wembley victory over Manchester United, but who were our first opponents in that season's competition?

7 There were plenty of memorable goals during the campaign, but the best was undoubtedly a 35-yard strike which beat Peter Shilton in the fourth round replay at Derby. Who scored that goal?

8 Perhaps surprisingly, our leading scorer during the League Cup campaign was not a forward. Who was it?

9 Back to the final: who was named 'Man of the Match' at Wembley?

10 Yorkshire TV's match coverage of the final caused great controversy in South Yorkshire. Why?

11 And finally, I'm sure many of you can name all of Wednesday's League Cup final starting XI, but can you remember the identity of the unused substitute?

## OWL-A-GRAM

*Unscramble the letters to find one of Wednesday's Wembley-winning wizards:*

# I AM ELDER WAND

# The Biggest and the Best

It's time to don your thinking caps now, for a heavyweight round on club records and feats. Given Wednesday's long history, it's unlikely that you'll be able to rely on first-hand experience to answer all of these questions. However, I'm sure a few of you will be great scholars of the club and know most of the answers and, for those that don't, it's another chance to learn a bit more about our great club's distinguished history. So enjoy, but if you don't know all of the answers don't despair – you're probably just too young!

1   A relatively easy one to start with: which left-sided Northern Ireland international is the Owls' most capped footballer?

2   And who has won the most England caps during his time as a Wednesday player?

3   The person who has made the most appearances for our club is a Scot who played during the first two decades of the twentieth century. Can you name him?

4   Martin Hodge holds the club record for playing in the most consecutive League and Cup games. How many consecutive Owls appearances did he make between 1983 and 1987?

5   The previous holder of this record was a diminutive winger who played 189 consecutive League and Cup matches between 1928 and 1932. Who is he?

6   Wednesday's record League victory was recorded against Birmingham in December 1930 – what was the score?

7   The only person to be named the Football Writers' Association 'Footballer of the Year' while playing for the Owls won the coveted award in 1993. Can you name him?

8   Derek Dooley famously holds the record for the most goals in one season. How many times did the prolific marksman find the back of the net during the momentous 1951/52 campaign?

9   Dooley once scored five goals in a game, but only one player in the club's history has ever bagged six goals in a League fixture. Who?

10  An unusual one now: Wednesday hold the bounce-back-ability record for regaining their top-flight status in the season immediately following relegation. How many times have we achieved this feat?

11  The Full Members Cup, in its many guises, did not yield much success for the Owls, but the club did create one competition record in November 1989. What was it?

## TAKE FIVE

*Name the five players who have scored the most post-war goals for Wednesday.*

# Twenty-first Century Owls

OK, when the historians are documenting our club history, the early twenty-first century will not be categorised as the 'glory years'. But, trying to put a positive spin on it, this period has at least not been as bad as the 1970s! And, while we may have endured our fair share of lows, those disappointments have been punctuated with the odd moment of triumph, if at a more lowly level than we would have liked. I'm obviously having an uncharacteristic 'glass half full' moment, so enjoy this round on our recent history which is packed with trophies, awards and achievements, some perhaps more coveted than others.

1    Who was our leading goal scorer during the 2011/12 promotion-winning season?

2    And which Hillsborough favourite was voted the PFA Fans' League One 'Player of the Year' for 2011/12?

3    Our best cup run of the twenty-first century was in the League Cup during the 2001/02 campaign. What round did we reach and who eventually knocked us out?

4 Which Scottish-born Wednesday legend scooped the
'Wash and Go' Good Sport Award at the 2006 Football
League prize-giving ceremony?

5 Continuing the awards theme: which Owls defender won
the coveted 'Wickes' Young Apprentice Trophy in 2008?

6 Danny Wilson was still at the Hillsborough helm as the
new century dawned, but how many people in total took
up 'permanent' residency in the Wednesday manager's
office during the first 13 years of the twenty-first
century?

7 In the first 13 seasons of the twenty-first century, only
one Wednesday player scored 20 goals in a season. Can
you name him?

8 Conversely, during the 2005/06 campaign, no Wednesday
marksman managed to get into double figures. Which
midfielder topped the scoring charts that season with just
seven goals?

9 Back to the glory moments: who scored our first
goal during the League One play-off final victory over
Hartlepool at the Millennium Stadium in May 2005?

10 And which team did we beat in the semi-final to set up
that Millennium showdown?

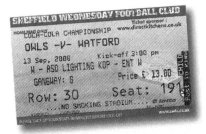

11  Finally, only four men from the Republic of Ireland have
    ever won Wednesday's 'Player of the Year' award and all
    of them did so during the twenty-first century. Can you
    identify any two of them?

## OWL-A-GRAM

*Unscramble the letters to find the name of a
twenty-first century Owl who bagged 17 goals in 62
Wednesday appearances:*

### LOUD OR MAD PACK

# Round

# 17

# 'We're All Going on a European Tour...'

It's fair to say that a passport and European atlas have not been essential items for Wednesday fans in recent years. However, the Owls have graced the European stage on four occasions (five if you include the Anglo-Italian Cup) and enjoyed some magical moments along the way. The club's first European match was an Inter-Cities Fairs Cup encounter at Olympique Lyon in September 1961, while our most recent European sortie was the 1995 Intertoto campaign. Anyway, enough chit chat, it's time to find out how much you know about our European conquests…

1   What is the furthest stage of a European competition Wednesday have ever reached?

2   Our record European victory came in a first round UEFA Cup clash in 1992. Who were the opponents and what was the score?

3   Two Wednesday players have scored European hat-tricks; one against AS Roma in 1961 and the other against FC

Utrecht in 1963. Can you name either of our hat-trick heroes?

4   The record for the most European club appearances is ten, held jointly by three Owls legends from the 1960s. Can you name any two of them?

5   In our 1992 UEFA Cup campaign, which player started all four games and finished as the club's leading scorer despite being close to death after being knocked unconscious in the first round first-leg tie at Hillsborough?

6   Tough one now: two fringe players made their
    Wednesday debuts in the away leg of our first round
    UEFA Cup tie in October 1992. Can you name either of
    them?

7   A lot easier this one: who gave us a fifth-minute
    lead in our second round 1992 UEFA Cup tie at FC
    Kaiserslautern before being controversially sent off?

8   And which striker topped the scoring charts in the 1995
    Intertoto campaign, despite being dismissed in our final
    group game against Aarhus GF?

9   The Owls were eliminated at the group stage of the
    Intertoto Cup, but where did we finish in the group and
    which German side topped the table?

10  Five 'guest' loanees played in the Owls' first Intertoto
    Cup match at FC Basle. One was a popular striker who
    began his career with Wednesday making over 100
    appearances for the club between 1980 and 1985. Can
    you name him?

11  Hillsborough did not host any of our Intertoto Cup games
    in 1995. On which ground did we play our 'home' matches
    and why didn't we play in S6?

## FACT OR FICTION?

*Sheffield Wednesday once beat Barcelona in a
competitive European game.*

# Round

# 18

# Who Gives a Hoot?

Apologies for the title but I thought you can't have too many bad Owl puns in a book about Sheffield Wednesday, can you? And it sort of fits with the theme of this round, which features an eclectic collection of semi-interesting obscure facts about our great club and the lexicon of players who have worn the famous blue and white stripes. So, without any further ado, pop on your most dapper anoraks and have a go at this lot.

1   Wednesday's first ever substitute in a League game appeared during the October 1965 Hillsborough clash with Sunderland. The player was a young Sheffield-born inside forward making his Owls debut. Can you name him?

2   It was one year and ten months after David Hirst's departure before another Wednesday player donned the famous number nine shirt. The new recipient made his debut against Liverpool in August 1999 and scored 43 goals in four seasons as the Owls slipped down the leagues. Who was the player?

3 What unusual goal-scoring feat did Andy Blair achieve in a 1984 League Cup tie against Luton Town?

4 A Wednesday player was shown two yellow cards during the October 2008 Hillsborough victory over the Blades but we still ended the game with eleven players on the pitch. Why?

5 The 1993 League Cup and FA Cup finals were the first to be contested between the same teams. What other footballing first occurred in these finals?

6 Wednesday's first appearance in an FA Cup final was against Blackburn Rovers in 1890. What was unusual about Blackburn's kit?

7 Which Wednesday stalwart of the early twentieth century has gone down in footballing folklore as the smallest goalkeeper ever to play for England?

8 And which Owls legend of the 1950s won international caps with both England and Zambia?

9 The first professional footballer to successfully claim compensation for a career-ending tackle was a Wednesday player. He suffered the horrific injury during an FA Cup fourth round replay against Chester City at Hillsborough in 1987. Name the player.

10 Which former Hillsborough favourite was harshly included in BBC Three's Worst Ever England Football Team?

11 And finally, which Wednesday legend once held the record for the fastest shot ever recorded?

## TAKE FIVE

*During the 1990s, five players scored for the Owls at Wembley. Can you name them all?*

# All the Glory
# of the Cup

The FA Cup is the most famous domestic cup competition in the world and has a special place in all football supporters' hearts. And we've certainly enjoyed our fair share of cup glory over the years. In total, Wednesday have reached the FA Cup final on six occasions, although a majority of those were quite a while ago; indeed, if I mention the '90s in this round I will need to specify either the 1890s or the 1990s – and there's a clue to the first answer for the eagle-eyed amongst you! Anyway, it's time to get out your rattles and wave your scarves as we revel in some of our magical FA Cup moments from down the years.

1   In which year did Wednesday first win the FA Cup?
2   And who scored both of our goals to secure that first FA Cup final victory?
3   Only nine players have ever scored in every round of the FA Cup during one season. Amongst this elite band of men is a legendary Wednesday winger whose goals helped us lift the cup in 1935: can you name him?

4   Which former Wednesday boss won the FA Cup with three different clubs – once as a player with Aston Villa and then as manager with both the Owls and Nottingham Forest?

5   En route to the 1966 FA Cup final, Wednesday became only the second team in history to accomplish what feat?

6   And who was the manager who guided us to the 1966 FA Cup final?

7   One of Wednesday's most memorable FA Cup moments
    was a third round encounter in 1979, when Jack
    Charlton's third-tier team captured the nation's hearts
    with a gallant performance in what turned out to be the
    third longest tie of all time. Who were our top-flight
    opponents and how many matches did it take before we
    eventually succumbed? (Funnily enough, this has also
    turned out to be the longest question in the book!)

8   Another memorable FA Cup tie took place in front of
    a bumper Hillsborough crowd in March 1983, with the
    Owls beating Burnley 5–0 in a quarter-final replay. Two
    players each bagged a brace during that game: can you
    name either of them?

9   And which team did we beat in another Hillsborough quarter-final replay, this time in 1993, to set up the prospect of an all-Sheffield FA Cup semi-final clash?

10  We all know that the 1993 FA Cup semi-final took place at Wembley. However, where was the match originally scheduled to be played before extreme pressure from both Wednesday and United fans led to the venue being switched?

11  Although it's fair to say Wednesday have not enjoyed much FA Cup glory in the twenty-first century, we did knock one team from a higher division out of the competition in January 2012. Which high-flying Championship side did we beat at Hillsborough in that third round clash?

## FACT OR FICTION?

*Sheffield Wednesday played in more FA Cup quarter-finals during the 1980s than they did during the 1990s.*

# Round

# 20

# A Cup Full of Woe

While the FA Cup has brought much glory for the Owls, we've also had to endure our fair share of cup heartache. In many ways, that's to be expected – we've entered the famous competition more than 120 times and, as we've only won it on three occasions, we've obviously had to suffer the pain and anguish of quite a few cup exits. Some of those defeats, though, have been harder to take than others, particularly those where we have been on the wrong end of a cup shock. So, it's time to commiserate with each other and console ourselves with the thought that there's always next season, as we meander down a rocky FA Cup memory lane.

1  Which third-tier team beat us for the first time in their history to dump us out of the FA Cup in 2012/13?

2  On only one occasion since the Second World War have Wednesday suffered defeat in the first round of the FA Cup. Can you remember which team inflicted that ignominy on us during the 2004/05 season?

3  It is fair to say that we didn't experience a great deal of FA Cup success in the first decade of the twenty-first

century. In total, how many FA Cup ties did we actually win during the ten-season period from 2000/01 to 2009/10?

4 Although Wednesday did lift the FA Cup during the 1930s, we were the victims of two big shocks during that decade. On both occasions local rivals who were struggling near the bottom of the Second Division defeated the top-flight Owls. Can you name the two near neighbours who beat us in 1931 and 1933?

5 During the 1963/64 campaign we finished sixth in the old First Division, but were dumped out of the FA Cup at the third round stage by a Welsh Fourth Division side. Who were those opponents?

6 Another Fourth Division minnow famously knocked us out of the FA Cup six years later. Can you name the team that inflicted a 2–1 Hillsborough defeat to send us crashing out at the fourth round stage in January 1970?

7 And which famous Wednesday defender made his final appearance for the Owls during that shock defeat?

8 In December 1977, we suffered another humiliating FA Cup exit, this time in the second round of the competition. Can you name our non-league opponents who sent us crashing out of the cup?

9 And who was our manager when we were slain by those non-league opponents?

10 During the 1987/88 season, Wednesday became embroiled in a marathon third round tie against reigning League Champions, Everton. But after three hard-earned draws we went out with a whimper in the third replay at

SHEFFIELD
WEDNESDAY

1987/88 CLUB SPONSORS   FINLUX TV & VIDEO

**V**

EVERTON

Wednesday, 27th January, 1988   Kick-off 7.30 p.m.   F.A. Cup 3rd Round, 3rd Replay

TODAY'S MATCH SPONSOR – E.L.G. HANIEL METALS     Price 70p

Hillsborough. What was the embarrassing scoreline in that final game?

11   An FA Cup exit was the least of our worries during the 1999/00 campaign, but against which club, that was two leagues below us at the time, did we concede three goals in the last 20 minutes to slide out at the fifth round stage?

## FACT OR FICTION? ————

*The team Wednesday have been drawn against most often in the FA Cup is Sheffield United.*

# Round

# 21

# In Opposition

Although I could be accused of bias, I think it's a universally accepted truth that Wednesday have the best away support in the whole of the country, if not the world. And this round has been written especially for that loyal band of fans that follow our great club to every away game. Listed below is the name of a ground along with a date, and all you have to do is name our opponents in each of those games. If you can recall the final score and the competition in which the game took place then you'll also be entitled to a smug sense of self-satisfaction!

1  Victoria Park, 28 August 2010.
2  Ewood Park, 22 April 1980.
3  Highfield Road, 6 May 2000.
4  Ayresome Park, 20 April 1974.
5  Fritz Walter Stadion, 20 October 1992.
6  Turf Moor, 26 April 2003.
7  Maine Road, 4 September 1979.
8  Abbey Stadium, 16 February 1991.
9  The Dell, 29 November 1997.
10  Highbury, 16 April 1983.
11  Recreation Ground, 3 October 1989.

## OWL-PHABET

*The names of four grounds where Wednesday played a League or Cup first-team fixture during 2012/13 begin with an 'S'. Can you name them?*

# Round 22

# Fledgling Owls

While some clubs do have the financial muscle to buy on-field success, a thriving youth system is usually one of the key ingredients to any club's prosperity. There are also few things that give a club's supporters greater pride than to see youngsters breaking into their first-team squad. It gives fans a genuine sense of optimism and hope that the future of the club is looking rosy. So, on that positive note, have a go at this collection of questions that all focus on Hillsborough's youngsters, both past and present.

1 OK, let's kick off with the obvious question: the youngest player ever to appear in a League fixture for the Owls is a goalkeeper who made his debut in 1973. Can you name him?

2 Much trickier one now: who became both the youngest player ever to appear in the Premier League and Wednesday's youngest outfield player when he made his debut as a late substitute against Wimbledon in February 1996?

3   The youngest player to make a first-team appearance for Wednesday in the twenty-first century debuted against Southampton in January 2007. Can you name the young Barnsley-born defender?

4   Wednesday splashed out £37,500 for a young Chelsea midfielder in October 1965, which, at the time, was a British record transfer fee for a teenager. Who was the player we bought?

5   We also broke the British record fee for a teenager four years later when a Scottish midfielder was signed from Aberdeen for £100,000. Who was he?

6   Another one from the 1960s: which 18-year-old made his FA Cup debut in the semi-final against Chelsea in April 1966 and scored the opening goal?

7   Back to the 1990s: which double-barrelled midfield starlet scored Wednesday's first ever Premier League hat-trick?

8   And which teenage sensation from the same era did Johan Cruyff herald as the next Marco van Basten after witnessing his Wednesday debut during a 1995 pre-season friendly?

9  Another tough one now: Wednesday have only reached
   the final of the FA Youth Cup on one occasion. What year
   was it and which team beat us in the final?

10 Sadly, just one player from that FA Youth Cup final team
   went on to play more than ten League games for the
   Owls. This midfielder also won a full international cap for
   Wales. Can you name him?

11 Finally, can you name Wednesday's promising Academy
   goalkeeper who featured in England's Under-18 squad
   during the 2012/13 season?

## OWL-A-GRAM

*Unscramble the letters to find the name of a big-
money teen star who came to S6 on loan during the
2012/13 campaign:*

### CHIN A MONK CROW

# Two of a Kind

Bit of a 'Bertie Bassett' round now; don't worry, I'm not referring to any long-lost relative of the former Blades boss of that surname, I simply mean there's some variety in the content of the questions – they cover 'Allsorts'. There is a bit of a theme going on, though, as each of the questions has two answers, hence the title of the round. Anyway, enough chit-chat, get your teeth into this lot.

1   'He covers every blade of grass out there, but that's only because his first touch is so crap.' Which future Wednesday manager heaped these words of 'praise' on which former Owls midfielder during their days at Southampton?

2   Two managers left Wednesday and then began their tenures in charge of their new clubs with a League clash against the Owls at Hillsborough. Can you name them both?

3    David Pleat's first two Wednesday signings were Mark Pembridge and Marc Degryse, but can you remember from which club each of these players was signed?

4    During the mid-1980s, two club stalwarts moved from Hillsborough to Charlton Athletic: one was a striker and the other a defender. Who were they?

5    Which two players arrived at S6 on loan to bolster the Owls squad on 25 January 2013?

6    Wednesday's one and only foray in the Anglo-Italian Cup came during the 1969/70 season, when we were knocked out in the group stages of the inaugural competition. But can you remember which two Italian giants we played during that tournament?

7    During the 1950s, a set of twins played in the same Sheffield Wednesday team. Who were they?

8    An easier one now: which two players scored our goals in the 1966 FA Cup final?

**Sheffield Wednesday Football Club Ltd.**

**RULES · FIXTURES · VOUCHERS**

**SEASON 1978-79**

9   A striker and a midfielder topped the Owls scoring charts with 15 League and Cup goals apiece during the 1985/86 campaign. Name them both.

10  Two Wednesday players were shown red cards during a feisty Championship fixture at Coventry City in November 2006: one was a winger and the other a midfielder. Who were they?

11  And finally, which two Owls players were selected in the 1979/80 PFA Third Division Team of the Year?

## TAKE FIVE

*Between 1990 and 1994, five Wednesday players were transferred directly from Hillsborough to Leeds United. How many of them can you name?*

# The Premier Years

Although in many ways it seems a lifetime since our great club last graced the top flight of English football, we were actually founder members of the FA Premier League. Indeed, the launch of the new top tier actually coincided with the last golden period in Wednesday's history; we were even considered serious challengers for honours during the inaugural Premier League season. So, let's put recent financial woes to one side and once more bask in the glory of our halcyon Premier era.

1   How many seasons in total did Wednesday spend in the Premier League?

2   Only one man played for the Owls in every one of those seasons. Can you name him?

3   Who scored our first ever Premier League goal?

4   And which player has scored the most goals for Wednesday in Premier League fixtures?

5   Continuing the goal-scoring theme: who was the last player to score a Premier League hat-trick for the Owls?

6   A tricky one now: we jointly hold the record for the biggest half-time lead in a Premier League fixture. Do you know what that interval score was and can you name our opponents?

7   Our highest goals tally in a Premier League fixture was achieved in the 6–2 victory over Leeds United at Hillsborough in December 1995. Can you name either of the players who each bagged a brace in that game?

8   Wednesday actually topped the table, albeit briefly, during one Premier League campaign. In which season did we enjoy that lofty position and who was our manager at the time?

9   And which manager was in charge of team affairs for the highest number of our Premier League matches?

10  Only two people have played every single game in more than one Premier League season for the Owls. Both of these ever-presents were defenders: can you name either of them?

11  And finally, during the 1998/99 Premier League campaign, three different players were all Wednesday ever-presents – an Englishman, a Dutchman and a Brazilian. Who were they?

## FACT OR FICTION?

*Wednesday's highest ever finishing position in the Premier League was third.*

# Round

## 25

# Between
# the Sticks

We all know that goalkeepers are a unique breed. They clearly
stand apart from their fellow men: they're made to wear
different coloured jerseys, they're the only ones who can touch
the ball with their hands in open play and, as the last line of
defence, they are obviously the most vulnerable. I therefore
thought this eccentric band of brothers fully merited their own
exclusive round of questions. So here goes, see how much
you know about Wednesday's super shot-stoppers. But watch
out, there are also a couple of closet custodians out there who
somehow managed to infiltrate the goalkeeping fraternity.

1   Let's kick off with the obvious question: who has
    appeared in goal for Wednesday on the most occasions?

2   The club's first million pound man was a goalkeeper
    signed from Glasgow Rangers for £1,200,000 in 1991. Can
    you name him?

3   Which keeper left Hillsborough to join Liverpool in 1983
    but never played a first-team game for the Reds?

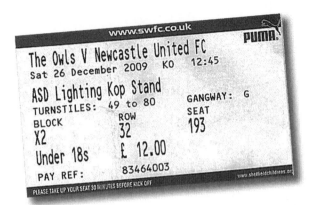

4   And which goalie, who Howard Wilkinson signed from Blackpool in 1983, spent three seasons at Hillsborough but never played a single first-team game for the Owls?

5   Two keepers were voted the club's 'Player of the Year' during the 1970s; one scooped the award in 1971 and the other in 1977. Can you name either of them?

6   And who was the last goalie to be voted Owls 'Player of the Year', receiving the accolade in 2010?

7   Which Wednesday keeper saved a penalty and then scored the vital spot-kick in an FA Cup third round penalty shoot-out against Watford in 1998?

8   Continuing the scoring theme, which Owls custodian grabbed a late equaliser against Southampton at Hillsborough in December 2006?

9   And which keeper scored against us at Hillsborough in October 1986, and who was the Owls goalie that he beat?

10  Which legendary Wednesday striker scored and then
    kept a clean sheet as emergency keeper in the 2–0
    victory over Manchester City on New Year's Day 1990?

11  Another club favourite also kept a clean sheet, this time
    deputising for the injured David Lucas in a 1–0 victory at
    Millwall in February 2006. Can you name him?

## OWL-A-GRAM

*Unscramble the letters to find the name of a
Wednesday keeper:*

### LICK SHARK RIND

# Wednesday Rogues

Like most clubs, Wednesday have had their fair share of colourful characters over the years. These loveable rogues are often the most talented individuals in the team who not only possess an inherent ability to perform moments of magic on the pitch but also a strong propensity to become embroiled in controversy. This round focuses on a number of those scrapes and misdemeanours which have engulfed our club down the years. But watch out, as well as featuring a few of Wednesday's most flamboyant performers, these questions also include the odd pantomime villain who's been thrown in for good measure.

1    Name the referee that Paolo Di Canio infamously pushed to the ground during the Hillsborough League clash with Arsenal in September 1998.

2    And for how many games did the FA ban the Italian maverick following that incident?

3    Terry Curran's dismissal during a Second Division League game in September 1980 sparked a riot at which ground?

4    And which future Owls striker was the other player involved in the fracas that led to Curran's red card?

5   In February 2013, Dave Jones was sent to the stands
    following a controversial second-half touchline melee in
    the technical areas. Can you name our opponents in that
    game?

6   Which on-loan player did Dave Jones label 'stupid' for
    getting involved in a Twitter argument with Owls fans in
    September 2012?

7   Two of Wednesday's 1963/64 squad were banned from
    football following their part in the match 'fixing' and
    betting scandal which was uncovered in April 1964. Who
    were they?

8   And who were Wednesday's opponents in the game that
    had been 'fixed'?

9   Which former Owls defender was charged with handling
    stolen goods after police found a safe from a post office
    raid in his garage?

10  'I loved the pubs. Lager and lime with a whisky chaser. I'd
    drink 10, 20 a night and then we'd train the next day. That's
    what England taught me, how to drink and play.' Which
    foreign import signed by Big Jack in 1980 uttered these
    wistful reminiscences about his time in Sheffield?

11  And finally, which bad boy of French football turned his back
    on Wednesday after declining Trevor Francis' offer of a one-
    week extension to his Hillsborough trial in January 1992?

## TAKE FIVE

*Name the five players who have made the most
post-war appearances for Wednesday.*

# They Came, They Saw, They Went

For a variety of reasons, some players have endured relatively short-lived Wednesday careers. This is sometimes because they're clueless, but it can also reflect cultural differences, a dip in form following their S6 arrival or because they are nearing the end of an illustrious career by the time of their Hillsborough bow. Anyway, whatever the reason, the answer to each of these questions is a former Owl who was signed on a permanent (if short-term) contract but who then went on to make less than ten appearances for the club. I know it's a tough round this one – so good luck!

1    Scottish international and former Blackburn striker signed on transfer deadline day 2002. Made four substitute appearances for the Owls totalling less than 90 minutes before being released at the end of the season.

2    Welsh international midfielder who won the FA Cup with Everton. Signed by Wednesday for the final two months of the ill-fated 1999/00 campaign; started the last seven games, but to little avail, before departing to Kidderminster.

3 Spaniard who arrived at S6 on a short-term contract in April 2005, was sent off nine minutes after coming on as a sub for his second appearance and never played for us again.

4 South African-born goalie whose only Wednesday appearance came as an 86th minute substitute against Burnley in 2002.

5 Tricky winger who came through our youth ranks and played six times for the first team before moving to Rotherham in 1988. Later played international football for St Kitts and Nevis.

6 French international defender signed by David Pleat in the summer of 1997 for £1.8 million. Returned to his homeland after much bleating and one red card in just six games.

7 Ghanaian international who began his career at Hillsborough. Made just three substitute appearances between 1997 and 1999 but, after a spell in the US, returned to English football and enjoyed some success with Bristol Rovers and Nottingham Forest.

8 Italian who arrived at S6 from Genoa in April 1998 aged 19. Scored a cracking goal on his Owls debut after coming off the bench against Villa, but featured just six more times before heading back to Italy the following summer.

9 Defender capped 100 times by Macedonia who joined the Owls in a big-money move from Hajduk Split in early 1998. Departed less than 12 months later after making just four Premier League appearances.

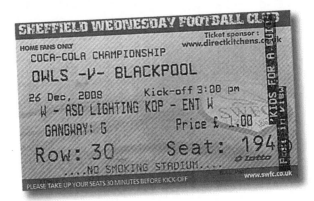

10 Won an FA Youth Cup winners' medal with Manchester United in 1995, but his career was in terminal decline by the time he arrived at S6 on a free transfer in 2008. Made just seven appearances in the Owls midfield before being released at the end of the season.

11 Jamaican international who made his Owls debut as skipper in a 3–1 derby defeat at Bramall Lane in January 2003. Made seven more appearances before departing to Colorado Rapids.

## FACT OR FICTION? ─────────

*Eric Cantona donned Sheffield Wednesday's famous blue and white stripes for one match.*

# Birds of a Feather

Another round with a bit of a twist now. This time there are three sets of five questions and all of the answers are the name of a former Wednesday player. However, in addition, the five answers in each set also have something specific in common with each other – hence the title of this round! I'm sure you'll get the hang of it.

*All of these ex-Owls were plying their trade in the Premier League in the 2012/13 season:*

1  An easy one to get us underway: Northern Ireland international midfielder who scored many spectacular goals during his three and a bit seasons at Hillsborough.

2  A bustling striker who arrived at S6 from Barrow in March 2003. He scored four goals in 30 Owls appearances before being shipped to Rochdale.

3  Trinidad and Tobago international who scored seven goals in

seven games for us during the 2004/05 season while on loan from Southampton.

4    Hapless keeper who endured a torrid 15-match loan stint from Middlesbrough at the start of the 2006/07 season. Wouldn't win any Hillsborough popularity contests.

5    Arrived at S6 on a free transfer in 2004 and made over 150 appearances in five seasons. Scored the decisive third goal during a 'Man of the Match' performance in the League One play-off final in 2005.

*Each of these players arrived at Hillsborough for a club record transfer fee:*

6    Careful with this one: gifted Italian who topped the club's scoring charts and won the Owls 'Player of the Year' award in 1999.

7    We broke the bank when signing this legendary forward from Notts County in 1951; indeed, not only did his transfer fee set a new club record, but he also became the most expensive British footballer of his day.

8    Central defender who made more than 300 Wednesday appearances between 1993 and 2001. Also won the last of his 59 England caps during his Hillsborough stint.

9    A Howard Wilkinson signing who spent just one disappointing season spearheading the Owls forward-line in the mid-1980s; eight goals in 44 appearances didn't prove to be great value for money.

10   Another Wilkinson buy who didn't live up to his big-money billing; this defender played 33 games during his one year seven day stint before 'Big Ron' shipped him off to Stoke.

*This group of players have all had loan stints at S6 during the last ten years:*

11  Midfielder who famously scored two goals against the Blades at Bramall Lane during his loan spell in the second half of the 2007/08 season.

12  Republic of Ireland international defender twice loaned to Wednesday by Bolton Wanderers, the first spell in 2004/05 and the second in 2010/11.

13  Scored four goals and scooped Wednesday's 'Player of the Month' award in October 2012 during his ten-week loan stint from Everton.

14  Another Toffee: this keeper debuted in a home victory over Southend in February 2007, that halted a win-less nine-game streak and then helped us avoid defeat throughout his 11-game loan stint.

15  And last but by no means least: soon-to-be England international goalie who kept five clean sheets during his nine-game Wednesday loan stint in 2006.

## OWL-A-GRAM

*Unscramble the letters to find the name of a famous Wednesday custodian:*

### SPORTING RENT

**Round**

**29**

# Sheffield Born and Bred

There are few better feelings for football supporters than seeing 'one of your own' make it into your club's first team. It's only natural that fans will have a stronger affinity with locally born players, and there is always a feeling that they tend to be 'playing for the shirt' that little bit more than the rest of the squad. Although none of Wednesday's current first team squad hale from the Sheffield area we have certainly had plenty of local-born heroes donning the blue and white stripes down the years. See how many of these you can remember.

1   Legendary Wednesday striker who topped the club's goal-scoring charts in five seasons during the 1960s.

2   Club stalwart from the 1970s and '80s who once scored 11 penalties during one season.

3   'Player of the Year' in 2011 after topping the Owls' scoring charts during his season-long loan from Preston.

4   Made just 20 Wednesday first-team appearances during four seasons in the mid-1960s, but then went on to

enjoy much greater success during his five-year managerial reign.

5 Promising youngster who captained England schoolboys to victory over Brazil; made his Owls debut against Liverpool in 1999 and played over 150 first-team games before leaving the club in 2004.

6 Made his professional debut with Wednesday at the grand old age of 23; scored 21 goals in two seasons, including our only goal in the 1986 FA Cup semi-final defeat to Everton.

7 Prolific marksman who scored 63 goals in 63 appearances for the Owls before his career was tragically cut short in 1953.

8 Teenage prodigy who bagged 65 goals in nine seasons before moving across the Pennines in 1958 for £45,000

THE OWL

Division Two
**Manchester Utd.**
Sat. 7th Dec. 1974, at 3 p.m.

Sheffield Wednesday match magazine·price 10p

which, at the time, was a record transfer fee between two British clubs.

9 More recent one now: reliable defender who scored a Hillsborough winner against Blackpool in 2007, broke his leg at Wolves a year later and also studied for a Law degree during his four seasons with the club.

10 Joined the club straight from school and became a crowd favourite during the 1970s; sinking to his knees, arms aloft as he celebrated each of his 66 Wednesday goals.

11 Another popular striker who made his Owls debut just 12 days after his seventeenth birthday; scored 27 goals during five seasons, including one after just 13 seconds of a League clash with Bolton in September 1982.

## OWL-A-GRAM

*Unscramble the letters to find the name of a legendary Sheffield-born Owls defender:*

### SMALL RED NET

# Round
# 30

# Owl's Well That Ends Well

Congratulations, you've made it to the final round! (Or if you're starting back-to-front, enjoy the quiz.) For this last instalment I've gone for a more light-hearted theme, as a reward for all your hard work – I suppose it's a bit like the last day of a school term when you're allowed to take your toys in. Anyway, no questions on nineteenth-century Owls, club record feats or even infamous defeats from the 1970s. Now I'm not promising that you'll get any of the questions right but – win, lose or draw – you will hopefully enjoy this rousing finale. And, as the great bard once said, that it will be a case of Owl's Well That Ends Well…

1   An easy one to kick off this round: which Wednesday cult hero from the early 1980s recorded his own version of 'Singing The Blues'?

2   Continuing the music theme, which injury-prone Owls midfielder from the 1990s is the son of a guitarist from a '70s pop group? (And an extra point if you can name the group.)

3   Not sure whether I'm now flogging the music theme to death, quite literally; but which '90s Wednesday legend was one half of pop duo 'Glenn & Chris'?

4   I'm obviously struggling to get off the showbiz theme at the moment so: which Wednesday striker from the '80s is married to *Men Behaving Badly* actress Leslie Ash?

5   And which actor, best known for his role in *Coronation Street*, is a renowned Wednesdayite? (And an extra point if you can remember his *Corrie* character's name.)

6   Talking about famous fans, which former England cricket captain is also a passionate Wednesday supporter?

7   And which member of The Jackson 5 is also widely rumoured to be a big Owls fan?

8   Getting back to football: to which famous game played at Hillsborough in 1972 does this apocryphal quote from father to son refer: 'If I find out you've been to school and not been to see Pelé, there'll be serious trouble'?

9   Talking about quotes, which ex-Owls boss uttered these immortal words: 'I never comment on referees and I'm not going to break the habit of a lifetime for that prat'?

10  And which former Owls sharp-shooter-turned-pundit is credited with these insightful comments: 'There was nothing wrong with his timing, he was just a bit late'?

11  Finally, which astute tactician and former Wednesday chief is widely attributed with this pearl of wisdom: 'I'm a firm believer that if the other side scores first, you have to score twice to win'?

## OWL-PHABET

*Four 'Nigels' have appeared for the Owls in a Premier League fixture. Can you name them?*

THE ANSWERS

# 'Hark Now Hear, the Wednesday Sing...'

1 Chris O'Grady.
2 Marcus Tudgay.
3 Just once; a 1–1 draw at Bramall Lane in April 1980.
4 David 'Bronco' Layne.
5 2001/02.
6 The 49,309 Hillsborough crowd was, and still is, the biggest attendance at a Third Division Football League game.
7 Ian Mellor, Terry Curran, Jeff King and Mark Smith.
8 Chris Waddle and Mark Bright.

GROUND | No. ADULT
650

FOOTBALL LEAGUE DIVISION THREE
V. SHEFFIELD WEDNESDAY
SPECIAL LEAGUE MATCH,
**CUP MATCH OR REPLAY**

SATURDAY 5 APRIL .80 3.00PM
**GROUND BRAMALL LANE**

ADMISSION
£ 1.30
(INCLUSIVE OF VAT)

THE SHEFFIELD UNITED FOOTBALL CLUB
LTD. DOES NOT GUARANTEE THAT THE
PROPOSED MATCH WILL BE PLAYED.

SECRETARY

**9** 17 – Wednesday lost Lee with a broken leg and had Pryce and Langley sent off, while Hedley and Bennett went off injured for United.

**10** Owusu made his Wednesday debut as a second half substitute in a Steel City derby, and scored with his first touch to open the scoring in a memorable 2–0 Hillsborough victory over the Blades.

**11** Quinn is the only player to have scored for both clubs in Sheffield derbies, with goals for Wednesday in January 2003 and the Blades in December 2005.

## FACT OR FICTION?

**Fact** – Wednesday and United were both in the Premier League for two seasons (1992/93 and 1993/94); the two Bramall Lane clashes both ended 1–1, while the first Hillsborough game was also a 1–1 draw and we won the other home Premier League encounter 3–1.

# Hello,
# Goodbye...

1 Roland Nilsson.
2 Colin West.
3 Regi Blinker.
4 Paul Williams.
5 Dunfermline Athletic.
6 Bradford City.
7 Gary Megson and Mike Lyons.
8 Barnsley.
9 Bury.
10 Red Star Belgrade.
11 Dan Petrescu and Emerson Thome.

**OWL-A-GRAM**
Andy Sinton.

# Round 3

# Cosmopolitan Owls

1 Siggi Jonsson, who was capped by Iceland during his time with the Owls.
2 Madjid Bougherra.
3 Benin – Reda was born in France and qualified to play for four different countries (France, US, Benin and Algeria), but chose Benin.
4 Norway.
5 Pavel Srníček.
6 Niclas Alexandersson in 2000. It may be a surprise to many, but Roland Nilsson never won the Owls 'Player of the Year' award.
7 Ola Tidman.
8 Guylain Ndumbu-Nsungu.
9 Gerald Sibon.
10 John Harkes.
11 Rodri.

## FACT OR FICTION?

**Fiction** – The great Brazilian did play twice for his club Santos in friendlies at Hillsborough; once in 1962 and again in 1972. However, although he did not score in his side's 2–0 victory in 1972, he did score a penalty during their 4–2 victory in 1962.

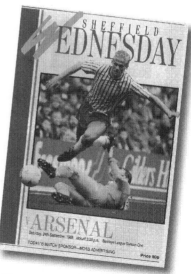

# The Last is
# the First

1  Peter SPRINGETT.
2  Orlando TRUSTFULL.
3  Miguel LLERA.
4  Gabriel AGBONLAHOR.
5  John RITCHIE.
6  Peter EUSTACE.
7  Etiënne ESAJAS.
8  Mel STERLAND.
9  Gilles DE BILDE.
10  Chris EAGLES.
11  Frank SIMEK.

## OWL-A-GRAM
Peter Shirtliff.

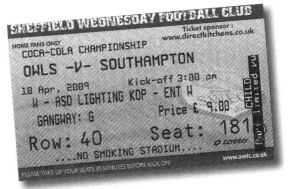

# Round 5

# In the Beginning

1  1867 (4 September 1867 to be exact).
2  The club gained admission to the enlarged First Division of the Football League in 1892.
3  Olive Grove.

**4** Although Wednesday moved to Hillsborough in 1899, the ground retained its original name, Owlerton, until 1913.

**5** The Cromwell Cup, which we won in February 1868 and which remains in the club's possession today.

**6** Three times: in 1896, 1907 and 1935.

**7** Four times: in the 1902/03, 1903/04, 1928/29 and 1929/30 seasons.

**8** Play was suspended after 79½ minutes on 26 November 1898 due to failing light. The remaining 10½ minutes were then completed nearly four months later on 13 March 1899; 29 players featured in this unusual fixture!

**9** James Lang.

**10** Andrew Wilson.

**11** 1929.

## FACT OR FICTION?

**Fiction** – Sheffield FC was formed in 1857, ten years earlier than Wednesday, and is recognised by both the FA and FIFA as the oldest club still playing Association Football.

# I'll Name that Owl in One!

**Player A**: Tommy Spurr.
**Player B**: Mick Prendergast.
**Player C**: Guy Whittingham.
**Player D**: Gerry Young.
**Player E**: Lewis Buxton.
**Player F**: Mark Chamberlain.

**OWL-PHABET**
Mark Smith in 1981, Mel
Sterland in 1983, and
Gary Shelton in 1984.

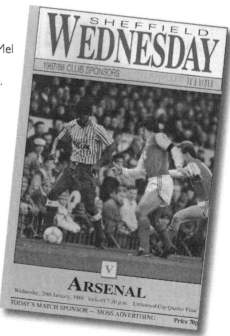

# Wednesday Till We Die!

1 Crystal Palace: the final-day draw at Hillsborough agonisingly left us two points adrift of Palace.

2 We lost 3–0 to Nottingham Forest, while Luton Town scored a late winner to secure victory at Derby County and send us down on goal difference. What was even more heartbreaking was that false reports briefly circulated Hillsborough at the final whistle suggesting that Luton had actually only managed a draw and that we were safe – alas it was not to be.

3 Manchester City: we lost 2–1 in a game that our opponents did not seem overly bothered about winning until an injury to Mike Summerbee fuelled City's passions and led to our 14-season exile from top-flight football.

4 A nervy 2–1 Hillsborough victory over Southend United in front of a 25,802 crowd saw us finish one point clear of the drop zone.

5 We beat Bolton Wanderers 1–0, thanks to an 86th minute goal from skipper Ken Knighton.

6 Jimmy Seed. We collected 17 points from our last ten games (seven wins and three draws) to secure our First Division safety and we actually finished in 14th place, although we were level on points with the six teams immediately below us in the table. That 'Great Escape' was made even sweeter by the fact that we then went on to win the League Championship in each of the following two seasons.

**7** Steve Howard.

**8** Eric Taylor: the Owls were relegated three times in total during Taylor's tenure (1950/51, 1954/55 and 1957/58).

**9** After eight defeats and one draw we eventually won our tenth League game, beating Wimbledon 5–1 at Hillsborough.

**10** Peter Shreeves.

**11** We only scored two goals in the final 17 League games. Our final points tally was a meagre 21 and we finished the season 11 points adrift at the foot of the table.

**OWL-A-GRAM**

Dalian Atkinson.

# Bouncing Owls

1 We beat Wycombe Wanderers 2–0 at Hillsborough, with goals from Michail Antonio and Nile Ranger.
2 Bristol City were our opponents, with David Hirst grabbing two of the goals. (Trevor Francis, incidentally, got the other).
3 Mel Sterland.
4 It was Sheffield United who finished third in the table by the slimmest of margins on goal average, which made promotion all the sweeter!
5 Harry Catterick in the 1958/59 season and Howard Wilkinson in 1983/84 – gold star if you got both!

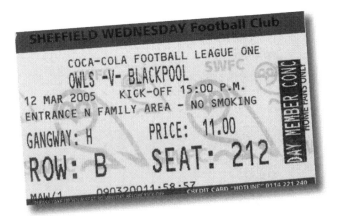

**6** Eric Taylor: we were promoted three times during Taylor's reign (1949/50, 1951/52 and 1955/56). Incidentally, this is exactly the same number of times that we were relegated under Taylor, in an era that is understandably known as the 'yo-yo years'.

**7** Frank Froggatt in 1925/26 and Redfern Froggatt in 1958/59.

**8** Mike Lyons.

**9** Roy Shiner, who scored 33 goals in the 1955/56 season, and 28 goals in 1958/59.

**10** Jeff Johnson.

**11** Steve MacLean.

## OWL-PHABET

Jon Newsome, Steve Nicol, Roland Nilsson and Ian Nolan.

# **Round**
# **9**

# **Connect Four**

## Connect 1
1  Trevor Francis.
2  Danny 'Agent' Wilson.
3  Derek Dooley.
4  Chris Turner.

**Connection 1** – All four men played for Wednesday and then went on to manage the club: Francis played 1990/94 and was manager 1991/95; Wilson played 1990/93 and was manager 1998/00; Dooley played 1950/53 and was manager 1971/73; and Turner played 1976/79 and 1988/91 and was manager 2002/04.

## Connect 2
1  Carlton Palmer.
2  Don Megson.
3  Viv Anderson.
4  Ronnie Starling.

**Connection 2** – They are the four men who have captained Wednesday in an FA Cup Final played at Wembley: Starling was captain of the 1935 winning team; Megson skippered the 1966 runners-up, and Anderson captained the 1993 runners-up in the first match, with Palmer skipper in the replay.

## Connect 3

1 Brian Joicey.
2 Gary Bannister.
3 Andy Pearce.
4 Dave Clements.

**Connection 3** – All four players arrived at Hillsborough following their transfers from Coventry City: Dave Clements and Brian Joicey arrived in a £100,000 'double' deal in 1971; Gary Bannister was signed for £100,000 in 1981, and Andy Pearce cost £500,000 when he was transferred in 1993.

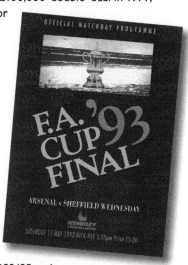

## Connect 4

1 Imre Varadi.
2 Gary Megson.
3 Jon Newsome.
4 Peter Swan.

**Connection 4** – All four players enjoyed two spells with Wednesday during their professional footballing careers: Varadi 1983/85 and 1988/90; Megson 1981/84 and 1985/89; Newsome 1989/91 and 1996/00; and Swan 1955/64 and 1972/73.

## TAKE FIVE

Des Walker (264), Peter Atherton (214), Kevin Pressman (207), Ian Nolan (165) and Graham Hyde (159).

# Who Scored the Goal?

1  Gary Madine – second-half penalty that saw us deservedly progress to the third round of the League Cup at the expense of our top-flight opponents.

2  Steve Watson – sweet volleyed lob from outside the penalty area that settled an incident-packed derby and sent Hillsborough delirious.

3  Deon Burton – second-half winner that extended our unbeaten run to ten games and kept our slim 2006/07 play-off hopes alive, at least for another two weeks.

4  Gary Shelton – memorable overhead kick that secured the points from the trip to Tyneside and kept our promotion juggernaut rolling back towards the top flight in 1983/84.

5  Imre Varadi – a brace that delivered our first victory at Old Trafford for more than 20 years, and started us on a mini-domination of the Red Devils over the next three seasons.

6  Lee Chapman – a late-headed goal secured a famous victory that ended Manchester United's 15-game unbeaten start to the season in front of an ecstatic 48,000 Hillsborough crowd.

7  David Hirst – our young striker came off the bench to score a spectacular late winner in another memorable Hillsborough encounter. And this was our fifth victory over the Red Devils in six League matches.

8  Nigel Jemson – headed goal that gave us some revenge in the return fixture against Ron Atkinson's Villa the season after 'Big Ron' had walked out on the Owls.

**9** Chris Waddle – famously managed to squeeze the ball in from a tight angle near the byline ten minutes into the game to secure victory at Elland Road.

**10** Lee Briscoe – a late, exquisite chip gave Briscoe his one and only Owls goal in 'that game' which we won 1–0, although I'm sure most of you will not have remembered either the score or the scorer: just Di Canio and the ref!

**11** Efan Ekoku – two goals from the Nigerian international, the second in extra-time, saw us progress to the fourth round of the League Cup at our old foe's expense.

**OWL-A-GRAM**

Nigel Worthington.

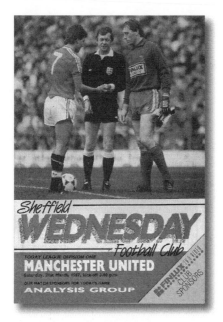

# Round 11 Just About Managing

1 Arthur Dickinson (1891–1920).
2 Peter Eustace: was manager for just 110 days, during which time we won just two out of 18 games (and one of those was against Torquay United in the third round of the FA Cup).
3 Harry Catterick: the Owls won 77 out of 134 games while Catterick was in charge (57 per cent).
4 Ron Atkinson (1989/91 and 1997/98).
5 Derek Dooley.
6 Gary Megson.
7 David Pleat's first game as Wednesday boss was the Intertoto clash with Górnik Zabrze in July 1995.
8 Terry Yorath was born in Cardiff and, although Peter Shreeves was brought up in London, he was actually born in Neath.
9 Chris Turner.
10 Paul Sturrock.
11 Trevor Francis (on four occasions, all in 1993).

## OWL-PHABET
Billy Walker, Danny Williams, Howard Wilkinson and Danny Wilson.

# Three Lions on a Shirt

1 Charles Clegg (he played for England against Scotland in the first ever international in November 1872).
2 Andy Hinchcliffe (hopefully this is not still the correct answer if you're reading this book in 2020).
3 Carlton Palmer.
4 New Zealand.
5 Ron Springett, Peter Swan and John Fantham – gold star if you got all three!
6 Ernest Blenkinsop.
7 Chris Woods and Carlton Palmer.
8 Des Walker and Andy Sinton.
9 Martin Hodge.
10 Albert Quixall.
11 Chris Kirkland, Anthony Gardner and Jay Bothroyd – another gold star if you got all three!

## OWL-A-GRAM
Chris Waddle.

**Round**
**13**

# It'll be 'Owl' Right on the Night

1 Nejc Pecnik.
2 McLaren scored at both ends.
3 Kevin Pressman – sent off after just 13 seconds against Wolves for handling the ball outside his area.

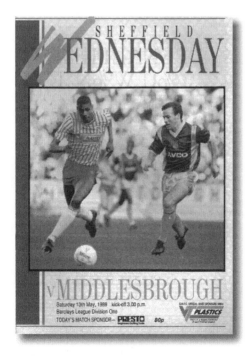

**4** The Owls became the first team in League history to score a goal without any of their players touching the ball after Fulham's Alan Mullery sent a 20-yard back pass into his own net after just 30 seconds.

**5** Mick Russell was the referee and he took down the number of Michail Antonio instead of Helan for the first booking – and we all thought only Graham Poll was that daft!

**6** Paul Warhurst.

**7** They all scored an own goal during the 5–4 defeat.

**8** He blew for full time when the ball was in the air from a Bolton corner that was then headed into the net. The 'goal' did not stand and the Owls won 1–0.

**9** Ten different Wednesday players all missed penalties during the 1977/78 season.

**10** Carlton was the first player to be sent off with each of the five Premier League clubs that he played for (Wednesday, Leeds United, Southampton, Nottingham Forest and Coventry City).

**11** Chris Waddle.

## FACT OR FICTION?

**Fiction** – The dubious honour of scoring the quickest ever top-flight own goal goes to Steve Bould, although the Arsenal defender did set the record while playing against the Owls at Hillsborough in February 1990. Bould managed to beat Gunners goalkeeper John Lukic after just 16 seconds.

# Wednesday Wonderland

**1** John Sheridan – I'm sure you can all still hear the 'dink' as the ball went in off the inside of the post.

**2** Rumbelows Cup – the now defunct electrical retailer sponsored the 1990/91 and 1991/92 competitions.

**3** Tracey Bateman, who was Rumbelows' 'Employee of the Year'.

**4** Peter Shirtliff, Danny Wilson and Nigel Worthington – gold star if you got all three!

**5** Carlton Palmer.

**6** Brentford.

**7** John Harkes – what a strike!

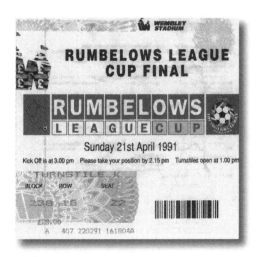

**8** Nigel Pearson, our captain and centre-back netted five times during the ten-game campaign.

**9** Nigel Pearson – leading goal scorer, Man of the Match; is there anything our super-human captain couldn't do!!??

**10** Instead of showing the post-match celebrations (as London Weekend Television did), Yorkshire TV cut the broadcast short in order to air *War of the Monster Trucks*.

**11** Trevor Francis.

### OWL-A-GRAM

Lawrie Madden.

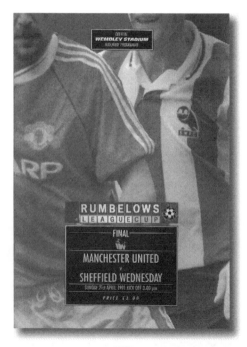

# The Biggest and the Best

1 Nigel Worthington, who won 50 Northern Ireland caps during his time with the club.
2 Ron Springett, who won all of his 33 England caps with Wednesday.
3 Andrew Wilson, who made 545 League and Cup appearances for the club between 1900 and 1920.

**4** Hodge made 214 consecutive appearances between 1983 and 1987.

**5** Mark Hooper.

**6** 9–1.

**7** Chris Waddle.

**8** 47 goals in total (46 in the League and one in the FA Cup).

**9** Douglas Hunt who achieved the feat against Norwich City in a Second Division game in November 1938.

**10** Five: in 1899/00, 1951/52, 1955/56, 1958/59 and 1990/91.

**11** Wednesday attracted the largest attendance outside of the final, with a 30,464 crowd at Hillsborough for the second round Zenith Data Systems tie with the Blades in November 1989.

## TAKE FIVE

John Fantham (167), Redfern Froggatt (149), David Hirst (128), Roy Shiner (96) and Jackie Sewell (92).

# Twenty-first Century Owls

**1** Gary Madine, with 18 goals.

**2** Jose Semedo.

**3** We reached the semi-finals of the League Cup in 2001/02, before losing to Blackburn Rovers 3–6 on aggregate.

**4** Lee Bullen, who was given the award for playing in all 11 positions during his first two years with the club.

**5** Mark Beevers, beating off stiff competition from Joe Mattock, who, at the time, was playing for Leicester City.

**6** Ten – Wilson, Jewell, Shreeves, Yorath, Turner, Sturrock, Laws, Irvine, Megson and Jones – but I'll also accept 'too many' as a correct answer!

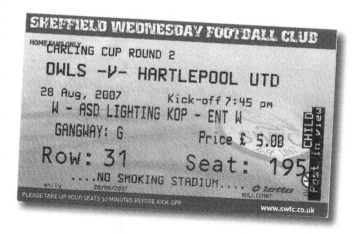

**7** Steve MacLean with exactly 20 goals during the 2004/05 campaign.

**8** Chris Brunt.

**9** Jon-Paul McGovern.

**10** Brentford.

**11** Derek Geary in 2002; Alan Quinn in 2003; Graham Coughlan in 2006 and Glenn Whelan in 2007 – gold star if you got all four!

## OWL-A-GRAM

Adam Proudlock.

# 'We're All Going on a European Tour...'

1  Quarter-final of the 1961/62 Inter-Cities Fairs Cup.
2  An 8–1 victory over Spora Luxembourg.
3  Gerry Young against AS Roma, and David 'Bronco' Layne against FC Utrecht.

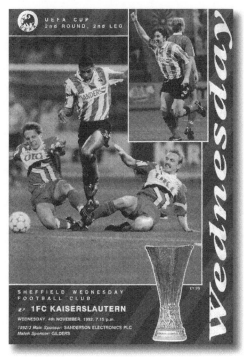

U E F A  C U P
2nd ROUND, 2nd LEG

*Wednesday*

SHEFFIELD WEDNESDAY
FOOTBALL CLUB
v 1FC KAISERSLAUTERN

WEDNESDAY, 4th NOVEMBER, 1992. 7.15 p.m.
1992/3 Main Sponsor: SANDERSON ELECTRONICS PLC
Match Sponsor: GILDERS

£1.20

**4** Ron Springett, Don Megson and Peter Swan each played in all ten of the club's 1961/62 and 1963/64 Inter-Cities Fairs Cup matches.

**5** Paul Warhurst.

**6** Julian Watts and Mike Williams made their Owls debuts in the second leg at Spora Luxembourg.

**7** David Hirst.

**8** Mark Bright.

**9** We finished second behind Karlsruher SC.

**10** John Pearson.

**11** Millmoor (Rotherham), as Hillsborough's South Stand was undergoing a face-lift in preparation for Euro '96.

## FACT OR FICTION?

**Fact** – We beat the Spanish giants 3–2 in the first leg of the 1961/62 Inter-Cities Fairs Cup quarter-final at Hillsborough, although it was Barcelona who ultimately progressed to the semis following a 2–0 victory in the return leg.

# Who Gives a Hoot?

1 David Ford.

2 Gerald Sibon.

3 He scored a hat-trick, with all three goals coming from the penalty spot.

4 Jermaine Johnson was sent off after being substituted. He received his second booking for reacting angrily to his substitution by kicking a water bottle into the crowd.

5 The 1993 League Cup and FA Cup finals were the first time that squad numbers and players' names had featured on top-flight English club shirts – although, yes I know, that doesn't make up for the results.

6 Blackburn played in a set of white dress-shirts that had been hurriedly provided by a London tailor due to a clash of colours – although, again, I'm sure it didn't make the result any more palatable.

7 Teddy Davison, who won one England cap against Wales in 1922 and was just 5 feet 7 inches tall.

8 Jackie Sewell, who won six full England caps in the 1950s and then played for the Zambian national team just after the African country had gained independence from Britain in 1964.

9 Ian Knight.

10 Carlton Palmer.

11 David Hirst, playing for the Owls against Arsenal at Highbury in 1996 with a shot timed at 114mph that hit the bar – I'm not sure the bar ever recovered!

## TAKE FIVE

John Sheridan, John Harkes, Chris Waddle, Mark Bright and
David Hirst.

# PREMIER LEAGUE

## Sheffield Wednesday
## V
## Liverpool
### 7TH AUGUST 1999

### SHEFFIELD WEDNESDAY

| | | | |
|---|---|---|---|
| Pavel Srnicek | 28 | | |
| Andy Hinchcliffe | 3 | | |
| Emerson Thome | 5 | | |
| Des Walker | 6 | | |
| Danny Sonner | 7 | | |
| Gerald Sibon | 9 | | |
| Petter Rudi | 14 | | |
| Niclas Alexandersson | 16 | | |
| Simon Donnelly | 18 | | |
| Jon Newsome | 19 | | |
| Gilles De Bilde | 23 | | |

### LIVERPOOL

| | | |
|---|---|---|
| 1 | Sander Westerveld |
| 7 | Vladimir Smicer |
| 9 | Robbie Fowler |
| 11 | Jamie Redknapp (Capt) |
| 12 | Sami Hyypia |
| 14 | Vegard Heggem |
| 15 | Patrik Berger |
| 16 | Dietmar Hamann |
| 21 | Dominic Matteo |
| 22 | Titi Camara |
| 23 | Jamie Carragher |

### SUBSTITUTES

| | |
|---|---|
| Kevin Pressman | 1 |
| Benito Carbone | 8 |
| Richard Cresswell | 12 |
| Lee Briscoe | 21 |
| Steven Haslam | 22 |

### SUBSTITUTES

| | |
|---|---|
| 4 | Rigobert Song |
| 5 | Steve Staunton |
| 18 | Eric Meijer |
| 25 | David Thompson |
| 26 | J Neilson |

**MANAGER** – Danny Wilson          **MANAGER** – Gerard Houllier

**MASCOTS** -     Chris Pigott (Sheffield Wednesday)
                  Melanie Wilkinson (Liverpool)

### TODAYS OFFICIALS

| | |
|---|---|
| REFEREE | G Poll |
| ASS REFEREE | G Atkins |
| ASS REFEREE | J Devine |
| 4TH OFFICIAL | M Halsey |

**SHEFFIELD WEDNESDAY
WELCOME TODAY'S MATCH SPONSOR**

**PETE OSBORNE LOGISTICS LTD**

# All the Glory
# of the Cup

**1**  1896.

**2**  Fred Spiksley grabbed both of our goals in a 2–1 victory over Wolverhampton Wanderers at Crystal Palace in April 1896.

**3**  Ellis Rimmer, who scored eight goals during our successful FA Cup run of 1934/35, including a brace in both the semi-final and the final.

**4**  Billy Walker, who was at the Hillsborough helm when we won the trophy in 1935. (He had previously won the trophy as a player with Villa in 1920 and was later manager of Forest when they lifted the Cup in 1959.)

**5**  The Owls reached the FA Cup final without playing a home fixture in any of the previous rounds. Only Birmingham City, in 1955/56, had previously achieved this feat.

**6**  Alan Brown.

**7**  Arsenal – with Wednesday eventually knocked out after five games: the first game at Hillsborough ended 1–1 with the same score in the replay at Arsenal, before 2–2 and 3–3 draws in the second and third replays, followed by a 2–0 Gunners victory in the fourth replay. The final three games were all played at Filbert Street, with all five games being played over a 17-day period.

**8**  Andy McCulloch and Gary Shelton both scored twice. (Gary Megson got the other goal.)

**9**  Derby County, with Paul Warhurst grabbing the only goal of the game.

**10**  Elland Road.

11  West Ham United; a late Chris O'Grady goal and a fine
    goalkeeping display from Nicky Weaver secured a 1–0
    victory.

## FACT OR FICTION?

**Fact** – Although we didn't get to Wembley during the 1980s,
we did make it to two FA Cup semi-finals (1982/83 and
1985/86) and two FA Cup quarter-finals (1983/84 and 1986/87)
during the decade. In contrast, we only played in two FA Cup
quarter-finals during the 1990s; one when we reached the final
in 1992/93 and the other a quarter-final defeat to Wimbledon
in 1996/97.

# A Cup Full
# of Woe

1  MK Dons, who beat us 2–0 in a third round replay in January
   2013. (They had previously not beaten us in six League
   encounters and one FA Cup game, although they had
   obviously beaten us in their previous guise as Wimbledon).

2  Swindon Town, who beat us 4–1 in November 2004.

3  We won a grand total of two FA Cup ties during the first
   decade of the twenty-first century: we beat Norwich
   City 2–1 in the third round in January 2001 and defeated
   Salisbury City 4–0 in a first round tie in November 2003.

4  Barnsley knocked out a star-studded Wednesday line-up,
   which included five England internationals, in the fourth
   round in 1931 and Chesterfield knocked us out after a third
   round replay in 1933.

5  Newport County, who beat us 3–2 in January 1964.

6  Scunthorpe United.

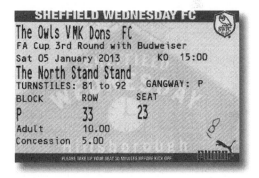

**7** Don Megson.

**8** Wigan Athletic, who beat us 1–0 in their final season as a non-League club.

**9** Jack Charlton, who had only been in the Hillsborough hot-seat for two months.

**10** A 5–0 debacle in which we conceded all five goals before half-time.

**11** Gillingham, who beat us 3–1 in January 2000.

## FACT OR FICTION?

**Fiction** – We've been drawn against the Blades six times in the FA Cup, although some of those ties were extremely memorable. However, the club that we have faced most often is Everton. We have been drawn against the Toffees on 14 separate occasions, including the final in 1966.

# In Opposition

**Round 21**

1 Hartlepool United – A riotous 5–0 early season League One victory that moved us to the top of the table.

2 Blackburn Rovers – Famous 2–1 victory in a Third Division fixture which all but guaranteed our promotion back to the second tier after a five-year exile.

3 Coventry City – Infamous 4–1 Premier League defeat which sadly all but sealed our relegation from the top tier.

4 Middlesbrough – Received an 8–0 drubbing in our penultimate Second Division fixture of the 1973/74 season, although we did ultimately avoid the drop; at least until the following season.

5 FC Kaiserslautern – A 3–1 travesty of justice in the first leg of our UEFA Cup second round tie.

6 Burnley – Defiant and emphatic 7–2 victory in a League One fixture the week after our relegation to the third tier had been confirmed.

7 Manchester City – A gallant League Cup second round second leg 2–1 defeat at top-flight City who needed two late goals from Tony Henry to knock us out.

**8** Cambridge United – A 4–0 FA Cup fifth round humiliation was meted out to Big Ron's team from a side one division below us at the time.

**9** Southampton – Memorable 3–2 victory in a Premier League fixture, which featured an audacious winner from Paolo Di Canio.

**10** Brighton & Hove Albion – FA Cup semi-final heartache as we lost 2–1 in Jack Charlton's final season as Wednesday boss.

**11** Aldershot – Handed out an 8–0 drubbing in the second leg of this second round League Cup clash with four goals from Steve Whitton, three from Dalian Atkinson and one from Craig Shakespeare. This set a record for the biggest ever away win in the League Cup's history, although, ironically, the first leg at Hillsborough had actually finished goalless!

## OWL-PHABET

Selhurst Park, St Andrew's, St Mary's Stadium and Stadium MK (Crystal Palace, Birmingham City, Southampton and MK Dons) – the first two in the League and the latter two in the League Cup and FA Cup, respectively.

# Fledgling Owls

1 Peter Fox, who was 15 years 269 days old when he made his Wednesday debut against Orient in March 1973.

2 Mark Platts, who was 16 years and 262 days when he made the first of his two Owls first-team appearances.

3 Mark Beevers, who was 17 years and 71 days when he made his senior Wednesday debut.

4 Jim McCalliog.

5 Tommy Craig.

6 Graham Pugh.

7 Chris Bart-Williams, who scored his hat-trick against Southampton in April 1993.

8 Ritchie Humphreys – after four goals in his first five Premier League games it looked like Cruyff's prophecy may come true, but sadly it didn't.

9 We got to the final in 1990/91 but lost 3–0 on aggregate to Millwall.

10 Ryan Jones.

11 Cameron Dawson, who made his England Under-18s debut against Italy in October 2012.

**OWL-A-GRAM**

Connor Wickham.

www.swfc.co.uk
The Owls V Coventry City FC
Sat 17 October 2009   KO   15:00
ASD Lighting Kop Stand
TURNSTILES: 49 to 80
BLOCK                    GANGWAY:  G
X2          ROW          SEAT
            32           193
Under 18s   £ 10.00
PAY REF:    72596003

# Two of a Kind

1 Dave Jones, about Carlton Palmer during their time at Southampton and, yes, Jones had signed Carlton for the Saints!

2 Harry Catterick with Everton in April 1961 and Ron Atkinson with Aston Villa in August 1991 (and, sadly, they both saw their new teams win).

3 Pembridge arrived from Derby County, and Degryse was signed from Anderlecht.

4 John Pearson and Peter Shirtliff.

5 Leroy Lita and Danny Pugh.

6 Juventus and Napoli.

7 Derek and Eric Wilkinson, who made one League appearance together in a Second Division clash at Sunderland in September 1958.

8 Jim McCalliog and David Ford.

9 Lee Chapman and Brian Marwood.

10 Wade Small and Chris Brunt.

11 Mark Smith and Terry Curran.

## TAKE FIVE

Imre Varadi in 1990; Jon Newsome and David Wetherall in 1991; Carlton Palmer and Nigel Worthington in 1994. Glynn Snodin also moved from Wednesday to Leeds, but in 1987. A whole host of other former Owls also ended up at Leeds (including Lee Chapman, John Pearson, Mel Sterland and Carl Shutt), but none of them were transferred directly from Hillsborough to Elland Road.

# The Premier Years

1 Eight consecutive seasons between 1992/93 and 1999/00.
2 Kevin Pressman.
3 Nigel Pearson, who scored in our first Premier League fixture: a 1–1 draw at Everton in August 1992.
4 Mark Bright (48 goals between 1992 and 1996).
5 Andy Booth against Bolton Wanderers in November 1997.

**6** We were 5–0 up at half-time against Bolton in the same match that Booth got his hat-trick. Incidentally, the final score was also 5–0.

**7** Marc Degryse and David Hirst.

**8** A four-game winning start to the 1996/97 season saw us briefly top the Premier League table under the stewardship of David Pleat.

**9** Trevor Francis, who was in charge of the club for a total of 126 Premier League games.

**10** Des Walker (in 1993/94 and 1997/98) and Ian Nolan (in 1994/95 and 1996/97).

**11** Peter Atherton, Wim Jonk and Emerson Thome.

## FACT OR FICTION?

**Fiction** – We did finish third in 1991/92, the final season of the old Football League First Division, but seventh was our highest ever Premier League finishing position, which we achieved in three separate seasons – 1992/93, 1993/94 and 1996/97.

# Between the Sticks

1  Jack Brown, who made 507 League and Cup appearances between 1923 and 1937.
2  Chris Woods.
3  Bob Bolder.
4  Iain Hesford.
5  Peter Grummitt in 1971 and Chris Turner in 1977.
6  Lee Grant.
7  Kevin Pressman.
8  Mark Crossley headed home a Chris Brunt corner in the 92nd minute.
9  Steve Ogrizovic, after a long punt out of his hands caught the wind and sailed despairingly over Martin Hodge's head.
10  David Hirst, although there is apparently no television footage of his goalkeeping heroics as this was the last English top-flight game not to be recorded by a single TV camera.
11  Lee Bullen, who replaced the injured Lucas just before half-time.

**OWL-A-GRAM**
Chris Kirkland.

# Wednesday
# Rogues

**1** Paul Alcock.
**2** 11 matches.
**3** Boundary Park, Oldham.
**4** Simon Stainrod.
**5** Brighton & Hove Albion.

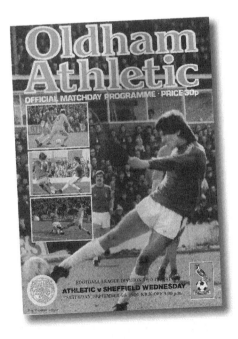

**6** Jay Bothroyd, who was responding to abuse implying he was not trying during the September defeat against Bolton.

**7** Peter Swan and David 'Bronco' Layne. Tony Kay, who had been transferred from Hillsborough to Everton the previous season, was also implicated in the scandal and received a similar ban.

**8** Ipswich Town – the game was a First Division fixture played at Portman Road in December 1962, which the Owls lost 2–0.

**9** Mel Sterland, although I must quickly point out that he was cleared of all charges.

**10** Ante Miročević, and the quote might explain why his Wednesday career never quite hit the heights that had been expected!

**11** Eric Cantona, and the rest, as they say, is history…

## TAKE FIVE

Alan Finney (503), Kevin Pressman (478), Redfern Froggatt (458), Don Megson (442) and John Fantham (435).

# They Came, They Saw, They Went

1 Kevin Gallacher.
2 Barry Horne.
3 Zigor Aranalde.
4 Sean Roberts.
5 Des Hazel.
6 Patrick Blondeau.
7 Junior Agogo.
8 Francesco Sanetti.
9 Goce Sedloski.
10 Ronnie Wallwork.
11 Darryl Powell.

**FACT OR FICTION?**

**Fact** – Cantona did play for Wednesday, albeit an indoor game. The six-a-side match was against Baltimore Blast at Sheffield Arena in January 1992.

# **Birds of a Feather**

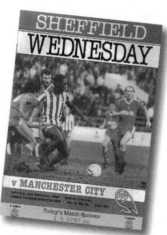

1  Chris Brunt.
2  Grant Holt.
3  Kenwyne Jones.
4  Brad Jones.
5  Glenn Whelan.
6  Benito Carbone, who cost £3 million when we signed him from Inter Milan in 1996.
7  Jackie Sewell, who moved to Hillsborough for £34,500 from Notts County in March 1951.
8  Des Walker, who arrived at S6 for £2.75 million from Sampdoria in 1993.
9  Garry Thompson, who moved to Wednesday for £450,000 from West Bromwich Albion in 1985.
10  Ian Cranson who moved to Hillsborough from Ipswich Town for £475,000 in 1988.
11  Adam Bolder.
12  Joey O'Brien.
13  Ross Barkley.
14  Iain Turner.
15  Scott Carson.

#### **OWL-A-GRAM**

Ron Springett.

# Sheffield Born and Bred

1 John Fantham.
2 Mark Smith.
3 Neil Mellor.
4 Howard Wilkinson.
5 Steve Haslam.
6 Carl Shutt.
7 Derek Dooley.
8 Albert Quixall.
9 Richard Hinds.
10 Rodger Wylde.
11 John Pearson.

**OWL-A-GRAM**
Mel Sterland.

**Round**
**30**

# Owl's Well That Ends Well

**1** Terry Curran, and it's still available to purchase at all good music retailers!

**2** Scott Oakes. His dad was Trevor Oakes, guitarist with Showaddywaddy.

**3** Chris Waddle who, along with Glenn Hoddle, released 'Diamond Lights' to an unsuspecting pop world in 1987. The single peaked at number 12 in the singles chart, and a clip of their infamous *Top of the Pops* appearance is, apparently, still available on YouTube. Google it if you dare!

**4** Lee Chapman.

**5** Thomas Craig and his *Coronation Street* character was red-haired mechanic Tommy Harris. (Incidentally, his stage name is taken from the name of former Wednesday star Tommy Craig – it is truly amazing what you can find out on Wikipedia!)

**6** Michael Vaughan.

**7** Jermaine Jackson and, although it is probably stretching the truth to suggest he's a confirmed Wednesdayite, he did once go to a Wednesday match (when we played QPR), so I think it's probably only fair for us to claim him as one of our own!

**8** The quote relates to the friendly with the great Brazilian team, Santos – Pelé and all – staged at Hillsborough on 23 February 1972. The game was played on a Wednesday afternoon and kicked off at 2.30 because the club was not allowed to use floodlights, due to energy restrictions caused by a national miners' strike. Despite the bizarre kick-off time, around 37,000 still attended the match, although official attendance figures from many local schools were apparently much lower than normal.

**9** Ron Atkinson.

**10** Mark Bright.

**11** Howard Wilkinson.

## OWL-PHABET

Nigel Worthington, Nigel Pearson, Nigel Jemson and Nigel Clough (although the latter did make just one Premier League appearance for Wednesday).